PROPHET IN PLIMSOLES

PROPHET IN PLIMSOLES

An Account of the Life of Colonel Ronald B. Campbell

by
John G. Gray

The Edina Press
Edinburgh

THE EDINA PRESS LTD
1 ALBYN PLACE, EDINBURGH EH2 4NG

ISBN 0 905695 04 6

Printed in Scotland by
Office Printing Services, Edinburgh

PROPHET IN PLIMSOLES

PROPHET IN PLIMSOLES

An Account of the Life of Colonel Ronald B. Campbell

by
John G. Gray

The Edina Press
Edinburgh

THE EDINA PRESS LTD
1 ALBYN PLACE, EDINBURGH EH2 4NG

ISBN 0 905695 04 6

Printed in Scotland by
Office Printing Services, Edinburgh

To my wife
Elizabeth

The royalties of this book are donated equally between
the General Council of the University of Edinburgh
to be used in connection with the Quatercentenary Celebrations
of the University, and the North Merchiston Boys' Club.

CONTENTS

Foreword

Edinburgh University has always had its personalities and characters and one thinks of Sir John Fraser, Sir Alexander Gray, Colonel C.M. Usher, Professor V.H. Galbraith and many others; but to one alumnus at any rate the 'noblest Roman of them all' was Colonel Ronald Campbell and we must be grateful to John Gray for finding time to write this book.

In the late twenties the Constable Report called for a number of changes in the organisation and administration of the Univesity Athletic Club and made the revolutionary recommendation that a Director of Physical Training be appointed. With wisdom and foresight the compilers of the Report stressed that the Director should not be a mere instructor but one who by tact and understanding could 'secure the confidence of the students' and make physical recreation available to a wide range of the University community. The announcement that the University had acted on this recommendation and had appointed Colonel Campbell evoked mixed feelings both inside the University and without. It was known that the Colonel was a distinguished soldier; that his training in the use of the bayonet was an experience few soldiers forgot; and that he had made a name for himself in Boys' Club work in London. How would someone with this background but no university experience fit into the student world?

The answer was not long delayed. The Director soon established himself and was quickly accepted by that most critical and demanding of communities, the student community. He began by placing on his office door a large notice bearing the legend: DON'T KNOCK COME IN and students responded by flocking to his office to discuss projects and problems. They encountered a man whose strength lay partly at least in his humbleness, sincerity, and sense of fun. 'I try to treat each student as if he or she were my own son or daughter,' he once confided to me and it was not empty statement.

His was the leadership that made each student feel that he or she 'counted' and was stimulated to further endeavour. Soon Minto House, primitive as it was, was radiating vitality, enthusiasm, and laughter and had established itself as a centre of student activity. In this and during his whole term of office the Colonel received much help from Mrs Campbell, who not only took an interest in the Women's Athletic Club, but opened her house to staff and students. Many will remember with pleasure and gratitude the hospitality they enjoyed in George Square or at Skipper's Cottage in Salen on Loch Sunart.

Ronnie Campbell had a deep sense of the 'sanctity of leadership,' a phrase used by Lord Linlithgow when he was Chancellor of the University. He felt that in the student community he had a unique responsibility to provide an example and inspiration, and the measure of his success is found in the loyalty and love he generated. He did not wear his religion on his sleeve, but he was a deeply religious man and one of his convictions was that health and spiritual well-being were inseparable. He preferred example to precept, but he could talk with earnestness and conviction on what he termed the 'simple fundamentals' of life. Needless to say such a man gathered round him a band of disciples of which the author of this book and the writer of the foreword are two. No one is better equipped than John Gray to write this chapter of University history and to remind us of a great character whose contribution to the University is difficult to exaggerate.

Neil Campbell

When a people begins to live on credit, on its past traditions, and does not pay cash down in energy, inspiration and ideals, it ceases to pay its debt to the world. It is only a matter of time before it becomes a moral bankrupt and is discredited before the other nations. This is no far-fetched theory open to doubt or argument; it is one of the most striking and relentless lessons of history.

R.B.C.

The red light of national decadence is material prosperity. The decline of a nation comes with the worship of wealth and the lowering of life's ideals, with ostentatious luxury and the insidious contamination of slums. No cunning use of rouge and powder will for long hide or stay the ravages of an internal disease.

R.B.C.

What is meant by fitness? It is something simple and concrete. A healthy mind in a healthy body - a moral force supported by physical powers.

R.B.C.

What is character? It is a combination of moral qualities which have the power to express themselves. Character is dynamic and not a storehouse of static ideals. Character is manifest in action. It must be built up by acts . . . the finer and greater the number of acts the larger and more noble the benefits.

R.B.C.

Introduction

Colonel Campbell was sixty years of age when I met him in Edinburgh during 1938. He came up quietly, as I was sitting on the floor of the old Minto House gym in Chambers Street, and invited me to join one of the physical training classes which he conducted personally on two evenings each week. Like thousands of others I discovered that meeting Ronnie Campbell was to have a profound influence on my life. Such was the attraction of his personality, even in his later years, that the greater number of his still active disciples must have come under his influence at a time when most men are thinking of retiring — if not already retired. It is a pleasant task to record this short account of his life and ideals. Colonel Campbell was a wonderful teller of tales and my aim has been to relate as many of these stories as I can recall. He was, however, a man of integrity and his stories are basically authentic, though like all great story-tellers, he allowed himself some artistic licence. Their purpose was to drive home some point he was putting over to the listener. It is a long time since I heard him tell those stories and it is now difficult precisely to relate each story to the original point the Colonel wanted to make. However, I have done my best to tell them in a context in which they will make sense to those who were honoured to work with him.

Although I have divided the available material into sections corresponding with successive phases in Colonel Campbell's career there is bound to be some overlapping, particularly as the Colonel had the capacity to undertake many projects at the same time. I also encountered the problem of dating activities which seemed to be carried out during successive periods of his life. I trust that any inaccuracies are of a minor nature.

It has been suggested that a modern appreciation should deal with the subject's weaknesses and not merely his virtues. This is an age of debunking and no doubt there were many flaws in Colonel Campbell's character. For example, in an age of technological advance he seemed to disregard mechanical aids, preferring to rely on the pick and shovel rather than on the bulldozer; or it might be said that his simplistic attitude to unemployment benefit is irrelevant in the complexities of the modern Welfare State. No doubt some of his ideas were politically naive and his social philosophy sometimes paternal. Lord Montgomery, who got to know the Colonel in the Great War, told me that his friendship with Colonel Campbell did not influence him in any way in the Second World War. Monty did not agree with some of Campbell's ideas but refrained from saying so because he regarded the Colonel as an enthusiast — a good thing in the Army, according to Monty.

Whatever may have been the Colonel's weaknesses he was a remarkable man. Those who came under his influence were left in no doubt that he had a magnetic personality. Of course he was an enthusiast — but only for what was worthwhile and creative. The man and his works speak for themselves. There is little purpose in scratching around to discover the pimple under the skin.

He epitomised the last great upsurge of late Victorian standards of conduct and voluntary service. After the Great War, thousands of men poured out of the Services with an urge to rebuild and found fulfilment in the Boy Scouts, Boys' Brigade and Boys' Club movements, as well as in bible classes, Sunday schools and churches. They had commitment, vision and ability. My generation owes much to their teaching and influence. The youth of the country still need the guidance of such men. The need if anything, is greater now than it was then. The problem today lies not in the rank and file but in their leaders.

Colonel Campbell received many honours in his lifetime. He was widely known and greatly respected. During the Great War he was a legend on the Western Front. As a sportsman he was acknowledged as an all rounder of exceptional ability, and as a sabreur he attained Olympic standard. His mind/body and spirit theory of physical education is now accepted by the universities, colleges and schools, as well as by many voluntary movements. Modern Army training methods are influenced by his teaching. His ideas on recreative physical training for the community have been widely applauded in principle if not yet universally applied in practice. His creative mind lives on in the Boys' Club movement, the Boy Scouts and in the Duke of Edinburgh's Award.

His researches into therapeutic medicine and industrial welfare now form part of the historic development in those fields of research. His detestation of tobacco is enshrined in government policy. Because of Colonel Campbell's modesty, however, his genius as a practical philosopher may not have been fully appreciated. Much of what he taught is highly relevant to modern living and should appeal to young people to whom he devoted so much of his life. This is particularly so in the emphasis he placed on voluntary service. Indeed there is a universality in his outlook that transcends time. His insight into life could well be described as a philosophy for survival and merits closer study by old and young alike. Much of what he stood for is now under attack — sometimes derided as being the values of a decadent bourgeoisie.

Nevertheless, I believe that his attitude to life will stand the test of time. In the end, that is what matters. Meanwhile, I have recorded his life and philosophy as accurately as possible, leaving it to the reader to judge the man and his ideals for himself — and to act on them if so inclined. That was the Campbell way.

7 Kilgraston Road   JOHN G. GRAY
Edinburgh
14th September, 1977

1

Early Life

The gas jets spluttered noisily and a smoky fire scarcely took the chill from the London office. The interview was uninspiring but the position was his for the asking. 'Well! It's at least a job!' he reflected gloomily, as he waited on the platform for the next train back to Bedford, 'but what a way to live!'

As he paced the platform he noticed a colourful poster advertising life in Canada. Towering full size above him an intrepid pioneer faced an enraged grizzly bear. Ronald Campbell stopped in his tracks. Deep in his memory strange forces were stirring. 'But of course,' he said to himself, 'Why not? My cousins are there already.'

The Bedford train steamed out of the station without him. Campbell was already on his way to the Immigration Office. The desire for adventure was too strong. He had irrevocably decided to go to Western Canada. The decision was sudden, but not surprising.

He was the second son in a family with strong highland connections. For generations its members had served their country at home and abroad. At peace and in war. His roots were restless. His grandfather James Archibald Campbell had held a commission in the Argyll and Sutherland Highlanders, and served the Empire in Queen Victoria's foreign wars. At the suggestion of the Duke of Argyll, he retired and took up work in Argyllshire, becoming Deputy Lieutenant, Convenor of the County, and Colonel of Militia. In 1832, he bought part of the historic lands of Inverawe with which the family had been connected since the fourteenth century. He farmed the land and built a mansion house which he called 'New Inverawe.' In the same year he married Jane Augusta, the daughter of Colonel Pocklington. James and Jane had six children of whom the third, Edmund Alexander Campbell, was Ronald Campbell's father. Edmund was also a soldier, serving as a Captain in the Indian army. On his retiral he became a Police Officer in Madras where he started the Madras Criminal Investigation Department.

Although most of his working life was spent in India, he took a keen interest in the well-being of the Highlands and campaigned vigorously for the reform of the crofting laws. He was popular in the West Highlands and became known as 'Lobby Campbell' and 'Crofter Campbell' for the enthusiasm with which he expounded the crofter's

1

cause. He married Margaret Eliza, a daughter of Duncan MacIver Campbell of Niagara-on-the-Lake, Ontario. Ronald was born at Ootacamund in India on 14th September, 1878. His grandfather died in the same year. The fact that Ronald's parents were both Campbells is probably coincidence, although, interestingly enough, the early Campbells of Inverawe almost invariably married members of other leading branches of their clan.

'Crofting' Campbell and his wife had six children, of whom five were boys. The only girl, Maria Grace, married Brigadier Carey and died in 1947, and one of the boys, Lorne, died in babyhood. When he retired from the Madras Police, 'Crofter' Campbell settled with his wife and young family in a house in Foster Hill Road, Bedford, where relatively inexpensive schooling was available.

He did not enjoy a long retiral and his widow was left to bring up four robust boys on a small pension. Life was hard for the Campbell family but Mrs Campbell was made of stern stuff. Ronald spoke of his mother with affection and reckoned that it was the discipline and poverty of their early life that produced a family of such sterling independence. The Campbell brothers were all strong characters, united in their love of natural pursuits. Ronald's eldest brother, Duncan MacIvor, emigrated to British Columbia where he became an authority on wild life. Edmund Alexander settled in Southern Rhodesia where he acquired two farms and an interest in a gold mine. He fought in the Matabele and Boer Wars. The youngest brother, James Archibald, qualified as a veterinary surgeon and became the curator of Toronto Zoo.

After the family grew up Mrs Campbell, who was affectionately known in Tamil as 'old woman,' moved to a delightful cottage in the village of Hardmead, not far from the Bedfordshire border. Ronald visited his mother regularly until 1907, when she died of cancer.

When the family settled in Bedford, Ronald was eight years old. Until 1890, he attended a private preparatory school called 'The Priory,' where his aptitude for games soon began to show. Although light and thin for his years he played full back in the school rugby first fifteen. The following year, he transferred to the now defunct Eastman's College in Southsea, which specialised in preparing boys for the Navy. He was a successful athlete at Eastman's but had to play soccer there, which makes his later success as a rugby player the more remarkable.

During the early 1890s boxing was introduced into the English Public Schools and in 1894 Ronald gave a good account of himself in the first Public Schools Boxing Championships held at Aldershot. In the same championships two years later he was defeated after a real punch-up by Ambrose of St. Paul's. The next year both boys met again in the finals of the light weight championship and once more hammered each other to a standstill, the verdict going narrowly to Ambrose. Whatever the attributes of young Campbell he lacked neither stamina nor determination.

At a very early age Campbell began to manifest the family interest in the outdoor life and his first nature diary begins when he was twelve years old. This keen interest in the living world around him was to be maintained throughout his life. Ultimately he became a recognised authority on birds and their behaviour as well as in many other aspects of wild life.

Ronald's success at games and his prowess as a naturalist were in marked contrast to his academic performance and he failed the Navy entrance examination. He then enrolled at Bedford College in the hope of following the family tradition by entering the Army.

There he took part in a wide variety of sports including boxing, track events, cross country, rowing, swimming, gymnastics and rugby, being in the first fifteen from 1896 to 1897. At Bedford he became Captain of Gymnasium and head boy of Ashburnham, one of the six houses into which the school was divided.

Not only did he play rugby for the East Midlands as a schoolboy but he was in the pack although he weighed (or so he used to say) only nine and a half stones. Such was his versatility that he played full back as well as forward. He also played for Bedford Town and subsequently for several first class clubs including London Scottish as well as Devonport Albion.

At the school sports of 1897, he romped home to win the open mile in five minutes three and a half seconds and later the same day was caught at the tape to come second in the open half mile with a time of two minutes twelve seconds. Both were remarkable times for a schoolboy all rounder of the day.

Bedford, like Rugby, bears a hallowed name in rugby circles. The town has the reputation of producing more first class players than any other town in England. Bedford's strength stemmed from the fusion of two strong local clubs in 1886. Colonel Campbell was a member of the fifteen which, in 1893, went right through the season undefeated. This fifteen, known as 'W. Ree's team' was a magnificent combination which has never been equalled. One of their great wins, was over the Barbarians, captained by W.P. Carmichael.

While playing for Davenport Albion he wore the red stockings of London Scottish which prompted the local Captain to say after a game to the Albion Captain: 'If you bring that red-legged b...... here again, we'll murder him.' This referred to his deadly tackling at full back. Campbell continued playing rugby until he was thirty and played against the first 'All Blacks' of 1905/6.

The first 'All Blacks' left a lasting impression on British rugby football. The team included some of the finest players of all time and their victories were overwhelming: of the 32 matches played they won 31. Later Campbell was offered a trial for Scotland but had to decline, having broken a rib when a horse fell on him.

At the end of his school career Ronald sat the examination for Sandhurst but was unsuccessful. Perhaps at that time too much stress was placed on a classical education. Ronald confessed afterwards that he had only scored 6 out of 100 for Latin! He then took a course in surveying but decided to join a maternal relation in British Columbria. While the lure of the Klondyke gold fields was the ostensible cause of his departure from this country, there was another reason. He knew that his mother was no longer able to support him and that he now had to stand on his own feet.

The dry range country of British Columbria is unlike any other part of Canada. The rain forests that clothe the coastal mountains cease abruptly a short distance inland to give way to open areas of grass, sage, tumbleweed and cactus. The valley bottoms support soft-fruit orchards and mixed farmland. On the sparsely afforested mountainsides, large herds of cattle are kept — the 'dry-ranges.'

At the end of last century, these forms of land-use were in existence supporting a sparse but increasing human population. Kamloops, on the trans-continental railway line, was an important centre although vastly smaller than it is today — 'the fastest-growing town in North America.' This dry, healthy, invigorating land of lakes, rivers and forests with its hot summers and intensely cold, dry winters must have seemed a paradise to someone with the energy and wide-ranging outdoor interests of Ronald Campbell.

A considerable proportion of the small population were British public schoolboys attracted by the grandeur of the country, the excellent climate and the tremendous sporting facilities. Initially, many formed what today is often called an 'alternative society' but most of them settled down and lived humble, isolated lives, supporting themselves by their skill with rod and rifle. Later they branched out into mixed farming and apple growing, while large-scale cattle-ranching boomed on the ranges. For a short period (until World War I) British Columbia was a rural Britain set in the Rockies and Selkirks. In 1914, the majority of those young men left their homesteads to defend their homeland. Few returned and the next wave of settlers took over.

This was the kind of life which called the young Campbell to the wide open spaces of British Columbia, and finally drove him to the Immigration Office in London.

His original intention was to reach the Klondyke goldfields but by the time he arrived in British Columbia the 'second winter' had already set in. The authorities were making certain that there would be no repetition of the grim tragedies that had occurred during the first winter of the Klondyke gold rush.

His relatives discouraged him from going further. He took their advice and got a job locally. For some time he worked on a cattle ranch at Cherry Creek owned by Bill Roper, one of the pioneer cattlemen of British Columbia. The old ranch premises are still there, although now incorporated into new buildings. The ranch is picturesquely situated in a wide grassy valley through which Cherry Creek flows into Lake Tranquille a few miles away. After leaving Bill Roper he became the factotum at Summit Ranch owned by a colourful Dutch American, Francis Allen, who was reputed to be on 'shooting terms' with his nearest neighbour. During the long fine summers he wandered far afield, bird-nesting, fishing and hunting. He learned to live rough in the open — an asset which was to stand him in good stead in the years which lay ahead.

For months on end Campbell's only companions were his horse and the animals which which he worked. This lonely life did much to develop Campbell's latent qualities of toughness and self reliance, while at the same time allowing full scope for the more contemplative side of his nature. Here for the first time he may have realised the therapeutic value of the 'power of the wilderness'.

He also worked as a bottle washer in a brewery and, with a gang of labourers, swept the sidewalks of Kamloops where he permanently injured his hands as a result of using a pick on frozen ground. The bottles were washed by filling them with water and then shaking them up with a pebble inside. The technique involved a short sharp 'jab'. Later when engaged in boxing competitions he found this powerful 'jab' invaluable in knocking out an opponent in the early stages of a fight.

When working as a cowboy, Campbell was initially laughed at as a greenhorn. His workmates, however, could not swim and confined their bathing to splashing in the river. It was a chance to get his own back. Campbell, an accomplished swimmer, dived in, swam under a log raft and then between the legs of three of them, giving Sam Roberts (his special enemy) a good pinch on the behind. 'Say!' quipped the astonished Sam, 'You got eyes like a fish! See under water!' After this the cowhands accepted him as one of themselves and Sam became his special friend and protector.

Another story provides a clue to Campbell's character. On one of the ranches where Campbell was employed, his mates were unable to ride the boss's horse as none of them could get a rope round its neck to take it out of the stall. 'Don't tell me you're afraid of that old nag,' said Campbell, 'You chaps keep out of the way and I'll saddle it up myself.' The challenge was greeted with derision. 'Don't you know,' laughed Campbell, 'that the horse is really a very stupid animal — watch this!' He then entered the horse's stall and for some time talked to the animal in 'horsey language' of which he was a past master. Then in front of the horse, he mimed the picking up of an imaginary rope and systematically went through the motions of putting it round the horse's neck. Opening the door of the stall he walked past the astonished cowboys leading a docile horse at the end of a non-existent rope. In this strange manner the horse was led into the corral, saddled up and gave no further trouble.

Although many of Campbell's Canadian experiences were to be of great value in later life, he entered his twenties as nothing more than a versatile youth with poor prospects. Society indeed might well have written him off as a late-Victorian 'drop-out.' While working in British Columbia, however, he had unwittingly taken a step that was to sweep him into a remarkable threefold career that was to change the whole course of his life.

He enlisted in the Nelson Rifle Company of the Rocky Mountain Rangers. The Nelson Rifle Company was one of several independent Companies of the Rocky Mountain Rangers, originally formed to deal with Indian revolts. At the time it was probably no more than another new experience for a somewhat frustrated young man, with a history of Army service in the family. By Campbell's time, Indian uprisings were a thing of the past and the only occasion on which he was engaged in 'Indian Fighting' was when called out to deal with a drunken Indian pot-shooting people from his cabin. Even membership of the Rifle Company brought him little satisfaction and he was on the point of resigning and becoming a professional boxer when he was caught up in the movement of events taking place nine thousand miles away.

2

1899 - 1914

THE BOER WAR

In October 1899, the Boers of the Transvaal and the Orange River Free State struck southwards to invade Cape Colony and Natal. They seized the passes, attacked the garrisons and then laid siege to the towns of Kimberley, Ladysmith and Mafeking. An army corps was mobilised in England and despatched to South Africa under the command of General Sir Redvers Buller. Offers of help poured in from the Empire and, on 20th October, Ronald Campbell enlisted at Kamloops in the 2nd (Special Service) Battalion of the Royal Canadian Regiment of Infantry. He was one of two volunteers specially chosen from the Rocky Mountain Rangers to join the elite Canadian Expeditionary Force and one of the youngest in the Regiment. The battalion was mobilised at Quebec and, on 30th October, sailed for Cape Town on the 'Sardinian' watched by a vast crowd of well-wishers. The vessel was slow and overcrowded but, throughout the long sea voyage, drill parades were maintained although in very difficult conditions. Unfortunately much of the drill consisted of manoeuvres such as forming square to repel cavalry — a military technique which had enabled British troops to cope effectively with lightly armed and undisciplined irregulars but which was to prove useless against the well-organised Boer commandos.

The battalion landed at Cape Town on 30th November and was immediately ordered to the front. Travelling northwards the troops soon experienced the realities of a South African campaign. After leaving Cape Town, the battalion was caught in a fierce sand storm and shortly afterwards a terrific downpour deluged them with their tents as yet unpitched.

On reaching the Orange River on December 7th, the battalion joined the Gordon Highlanders with whom they were later to be closely connected. At this first meeting reinforcements were urgently required by Lord Methuen at the Modder River. There was only one train available and it was a question of which battalion should move up to support Lord Methuen. Once again Campbell was gently nudged by fate. The Royal Canadians were directed to remain and devote themselves to much needed training combined with outpost duties. The Gordons entrained for Magersfontein — and disaster.

During Black Week, December 1899, divisions of General Buller's

Army Corps attempted to relieve Kimberley, Ladysmith and Mafeking but each relief column was decimated by the Boers. These defeats shattered British complacency and galvanised the country into action. Fresh troops were despatched under Field Marshall Lord Roberts, the hero of the Afghan War, with Lord Kitchener, the conqueror of the Sudan, as his Chief-of-Staff.

Lord Roberts arrived at Cape Town on the 'Dunnottar Castle' at the beginning of January, 1900, and immediately began to assemble a large army at the Orange River. By 12th February the Canadian battalion was on its way to join Lord Roberts' Army where it became part of the newly formed 19th Brigade under the command of Major General Smith-Dorrien. The Brigade comprised the Royal Canadian Regiment, the Gordon Highlanders, Duke of Cornwall's Light Infantry and the King's Own Shropshire Light Infantry. This Brigade, together with the Highland Brigade under Major General Hector Macdonald made up the 9th Division. In the subsequent campaign the 9th Division formed part of the main army under Lord Roberts. The Army consisted of 35,000 troops and 25,000 animals, together with a large number of supporting units.

Under the leadership of Lord Roberts it now abandoned its base, left the railway, and marched northwards towards Pretoria, the capital of the Transvaal. Bloemfontein, the capital of the Free State was taken on 13th March. Kimberley and Ladysmith were then relieved and finally Mafeking on 17th May. Three weeks later Lord Roberts entered Pretoria. The triumphant march into Pretoria took place on 5th June, led by the 19th Brigade. At the head of the Brigade was the Royal Canadian Regiment.

The Boers, however, were consummate masters of war on a small scale and their energy, skill and resourcefulness enabled them to carry on brilliant guerilla warfare until the signing of a peace treaty on 31st May, 1902.

Ronald Campbell took to war like a duck to water. He marched and fought with the Canadians over two thousand miles before being commissioned into the Duke of Cornwall's Light Infantry. Lord Roberts' march from the Orange River to Pretoria was the last of the great military land expeditions which had so often fired the imagination of Victorian Britain. In one epic march Lord Roberts had fought his way over three hundred miles to the enemy capital. It rivalled his march from Kabul to Kandahar twenty years earlier when he had covered three hundred miles in twenty-four days but with a hand-picked flying column of 10,000 men. Never again would a western army depend for massive troop movements on the legs of men and beast alone. The conditions were enough to daunt the most courageous. The troops marched for days on end, sometimes without boots and often in rags. They were beset by flies, heat, dust, stink and thirst and continually harassed by marauding Boers. Campbell's best friend was killed in mid-sentence — a Boer bullet between the eyes.

The primitive hospital conditions were equally appalling. Typhoid patients without nurses, untrained soldiers acting as orderlies, dying men in bell tents with thick clusters of flies swarming over their faces. More men died from infection than from wounds.

Although the war was bitterly fought, it was unique in the spirit of chivalry which, even in the darkest moments, was never quite extinguished. An abandoned wounded soldier was carefully looked after by the other side and truces were observed to succour the wounded, bury the dead or even to enable thirsty troops to fill their canteens with water.

Campbell saw the chivalry and the heroics and much of the vicious fighting. He was present at the Battle of Paardeberg on 27th February, 1900, when after ten days of heavy action the Royal Canadians undertook to achieve a decisive decision on the anniversary of Majuba Hill when the Boers had decisively defeated the British nineteen years earlier. In the dark of early morning, the Canadians advanced to within sixty yards of the Boer trenches before a withering fire compelled them to lie flat. In spite of their hopeless position, they kept up the attack for two hours and later in the day the Boers facing them raised white flags above their trenches.

He took part in operations at Poplar Grove, at Dreifontein, Thaba Mountain, Zand River and in all the heavy fighting up to the capture of Pretoria. About this time he was promoted to Lance Corporal. After Pretoria he was engaged in field operations against the elusive Boers until the end of the war. This involved skirmishes in the Transvaal east and west of Pretoria and also in Cape Colony. Corporal Campbell so distinguished himself in action that on 31st October, 1900, he was commissioned on the field as a Second Lieutenant in the Duke of Cornwall's Light Infantry. From then on he was a regular officer in the Imperial Forces.

Campbell was one of a number of N.C.O.'s serving with the Canadian contingent who were commissioned by Lord Roberts on the personal recommendations of their Commanding Officer. The views of Lord Roberts as to the qualities of character which were expected from an officer were well known and the commissioning of Colonel Campbell at the early age of twenty-two, gives some indication of the maturity which he had by then attained and the regard in which he was held by his superiors.

'In addition to military knowledge and experience,' said Lord Roberts, 'there must be good judgment, sound commonsense, tenacity of purpose, quickness of perception, promptitude of decision and, above all, an infinite capacity for taking pains!'

In Africa Ronald Campbell experienced much that he was to expand and develop during the next fifty years. In the Boer War, man still dominated events and many actions were determined by qualities of leadership and personal example. The long marches and the nature of the campaigns enabled him to study at close quarters the reactions of men under stress.

Roberts and Kitchener were both men cast in the heroic mould although each was the antithesis of the other. Roberts had great concern for the welfare of his men and led his army by winning their affection. By contrast, Kitchener pursued his military objectives at whatever sacrifice of human life he believed necessary. But there were others, such as that prince of infantry commanders, General Hector Macdonald, who took over command of the Highland Brigade after the death of the much loved General 'Andy' Wauchope at Magersfontein during October, 1899, and who commanded the Highland Brigade on the march to Pretoria.

Unlike Kitchener, Hector Macdonald knew his officers and got to know as many N.C.O.'s and men as possible. He inspected cookhouses, made sure his men were properly fed, examined a platoon's boots, took an interest in his men's recreational activities and looked after their health. He inspired his troops with look, word and action and they would have followed him to his death. When Hector Macdonald committed suicide in 1903 he was buried in the Dean Cemetery in Edinburgh. For days afterwards visitors came to his grave from all over the world and on the first Sunday after the funeral the cemetery became the centre of a vast national pilgrimage. During the short space of six hours it was visited by at least 30,000 people.

Ronald Campbell was a junior officer when General Macdonald was at the height of his career, but had Macdonald lived he was still young enough to have commanded an army in the Great War. Unlike Haig and French, he was an infantry soldier and understood infantry fighting. Many of the mistakes of the senior generals of the Great War sprang from the fact that they were cavalrymen or gunners with little practical knowledge of infantry tactics and conditions. The shortage of experienced infantry Generals was to have disastrous consequences for the youth of Britain in the grim days to come.

At the relief of Mafeking Lieutenant Campbell rubbed shoulders with the legendary General Baden Powell. Although the two men did not meet at the time they later became firm friends and both subsequently played a vital part in the shaping of twentieth century Britain. Nor was leadership lacking among the Boers. Comparatively small and ill-equipped commandos were kept together and inspired by the sheer moral force of some of their great commanders.

There was, for example, that incredible Battle of Spion Kop early in 1900. On the night of January 23/24, the British took what they thought was the summit of a mountain known as Tabanyawa, fifteen miles from Ladysmith, under siege by the Boers since October. Unfortunately when the mists cleared in the morning only part of the summit had been taken and the troops came under a murderous Boer fire from three directions at once. Desperate fighting went on all day. By nightfall thousands of panic stricken men lay amid the dead and dying on the summit with scarcely any shelter from the deadly fire. Savage, British counter-attacks had equally reduced the Boers to a state of desperation. The wounded were covered with flies attracted by the smell of blood. There was no water or food. Both sides were exhausted. As darkness fell the summit was gradually deserted by friend and foe alike. As the British descended, an ineffectual attempt to halt them was made by their Commanding Officer but the retreat continued. On the other side of the mountain mud-encrusted Lois Botha, arriving too late for the main engagement, cursed his fleeing kinsmen back on to the deserted summit. As the morning mists cleared Botha looked down at the incredible sight of an entire British army preparing to withdraw.

Finally there was General Sir Horace Smith-Dorrien who commanded the 19th Brigade from February, 1900. General Smith-Dorrien was born on 26th May, 1858 and had commanded the 2nd Brigade at the Battle of Omdurman. By now he was forty years of age and still a bachelor. He was adept at every form of sport as well as being an excellent shot. A man of great courage and modesty, he was held in the highest regard by the commanders with whom he served. The conditions under which he took command of the Brigade are in themselves evidence of the sterling qualities of the new Commander.

To join the 19th Brigade which was gathering at the Orange River, Smith-Dorrien rode 87 miles through country in which no solitary horseman was safe and was fortunate indeed in finding a body of mounted infantry headed in the same direction. The journey took five days through veldt inches deep in locusts. With every stride the horrible insects flew into the rider's face and the journey became a nightmare.

On taking over the 19th Brigade at the Orange River he found a scene of utter confusion, with masses of men, guns, horses, and oxen trying to sort themselves out into formations and units. Such a robust character must have greatly influenced young Campbell at an impressionable age.

General Smith-Dorrien's path was to cross Campbell's more than once in the years that were to come. In 1907 he moved into Government House at Aldershot. The G.O.C. made the barracks more attractive and provided healthy recreation for the off-duty soldier. Every piece of ground large enough for cricket, football and hockey was levelled and grassed and the general playing field area increased by fifteen per cent. Cross country running was introduced and squash courts constructed. When the Royal Engineers claimed that some trees would take weeks to cut down, Smith-Dorrien brought them down in six hours using a technique that Campbell was to employ years later when building a boys' club hut at Carfin Hall near Motherwell.

In the early days of the Great War, Smith-Dorrien commanded the 2nd Corps in its push in Belgium. At the battle of Le Cateaux, he disobeyed orders to retreat and held the advancing Germans long enough to stop the orderly retreat from Mons becoming a rout.

In his subsequent studies on the attributes of leadership, Colonel Campbell was clearly influenced by his first hand experience during the Boer War, and by the personal qualities of the men with whom he came into contact. Many of his views on the care of the body and on such topics as courage and chivalry, and the handling of people under stress, reveal the effect of the Boer War.

Nor did it go unnoticed by Campbell that many of the leading commanders of the era were far from young men. Lord Roberts was in his mid-sixties when he set off from the Orange River on the march to Pretoria. Some thirty-two years earlier, the massive punitory expedition from Zula on the Red Sea to Ethiopia had been commanded by the most outstanding soldier of the day — Field Marshall Lord Napier who was then in his prime at fifty seven years of age. Smith-Dorrien was over forty when he took command of the 19th Brigade. As Campbell's conception of physical fitness began to emerge as a coherent system he placed great emphasis on fitness for all ages. In his later years as Director of Physical Education at Edinburgh University, he personally conducted a special class for the over-sixties.

Colonel Campbell recounted many stories of his period of service in South Africa. When in charge of a blockhouse which was one of a number covering crossings on a river which obstructed the advancing Boers, he became involved in a ploy which may well have saved his life and that of his companions. Guard duty in a blockhouse involved long monotonous hours of watching interspersed with occasional periods of sharp action. To maintain the morale of the men under his command, Colonel Campbell took them out looking for bird's nests. Arranging his men in an extended line he moved slowly across the veldt. Whoever spotted a nest held up his hand and his companions gathered round while Campbell discussed the bird and its habits. This went on for many weeks. As time wore on all the blockhouses guarding the river crossings were taken by the Boers with the exception of that commanded by Campbell. The tide of war then turned and the British swept forward and captured many Boer prisoners. Afterwards the British entertained their captured enemies and Campbell asked the Boer Commander why his blockhouse had never been attacked. 'Ah,' said the Boer Commander, 'we are not fools, we had you under observation all the time and knew what you were up to.' 'What the devil did you think we were up to?' queried the Colonel. 'We saw you sow mines,' said the Boer. 'We were not so foolish as to attack.'

Another Campbell story is what he called the unwritten history of how De Wet escaped through Oliphant Nek. In June 1900, Christian De Wet, with many leading Boers and substantial forces, had escaped a British trap in the Brandwater Basin on the Natal Border. De Wet had been at large for three months with the exhausted British constantly at his heels. Finally, in mid-August, De Wet headed for a pass in the Mageliesberg called 'Oliphants Nek,' the gateway to Rustenburg. Forces under the command of Hamilton, Kitchener and Methuen immediately moved to block the three exits from the pass. According to the historians, Methuen got there all right but Hamilton was too late and De Wet escaped, closely pursued by Kitchener. Colonel Campbell regarded the official story as being something of a cover up. The 'Campbell' version of the incident runs something like this! De Wet was in fact trapped and would have been forced to surrender but for a completely unforeseen mishap. British troops, after days of forced marching, arrived at one of the entrances to the pass as De Wet was heading for freedom. The gun teams swung round to take up position and soldiers began to dig emplacements. Within minutes the guns would have covered the exit from the pass and De Wet's position would be hopeless. At this critical moment some luckless trooper drove his pick into a hornet's nest and 'away went the horses chased by the hornets and away went the guns after the horses, and away went the troopers after the guns — and away went old De Wet to harass the British troops for another year.'

This story illustrates how trivial incidents can alter the course of history. 'Did I ever tell you about the bravest man I ever met,' was another hardy annual. The company had been pinned down all day. The heat was intense; water exhausted. They were on the point of mounting a hopeless bayonet charge, when relief came from a most unexpected quarter. The regimental cook — a civilian who had never fired a shot in anger — was watching from a nearby hill and realised the danger. Festooned with reserve ammunition pouches, he was now bellying his way towards his beleaguered companions. He finally reached the Canadian positions, miraculously unscathed by a barrage of hostile rifle fire. With the arrival of the ammunition, the Company cleared the way forward with a successful counter attack. Remarkable qualities are often latent in the most ordinary of men. Ronnie Campbell believed that most of us have unsuspected depths of intelligence, courage and creativity. It only requires the correct stimulus to activate those attributes for the benefit of the community. His life was devoted to bringing the best out of those who came under his influence.

THE EDWARDIAN PEACE

The Boer War ended on 31st May, 1902 and Campbell was promoted to the rank of Lieutenant on 12th August. After the war he suffered from the effects of dysentery and spent much of 1903 on sick leave in Devon where he took the opportunity of doing some intensive bird nesting on Dartmoor. In the autumn he returned to Canada where, as a veteran, he was entitled to a grant of land on which to farm.

For a short time he returned to his old style of life and lived at Kamloops where he earned a living shooting wild fowl and killing coyotes for the bounty. However the call of army life was too strong and he sold his land option and returned to Great Britain and his commission in the Regular Army.

Life in the British Army before the Great War was very different from what it is now. The era of the 'Professionals' had not yet dawned, and the life of an officer revolved round tradition and etiquette, with plenty of home leave or absence on special duties. Many officers came from wealthy families but some, like Ronald Campbell, had to manage on their Army pay. He found it a hard struggle to keep up appearances in a good regiment. When in Devonport he made a considerable detour daily on foot to avoid paying a half penny toll at a bridge.

War was soon forgotten as the country drank the heady wine of the Edwardian peace. The motor car, the bicycle, the electric lamp, the balloon and the flying machine were new and exciting toys. The twentieth century ushered in the golden age of amateur sport with emphasis on athletics, rowing, cricket, boxing and tennis. The dreadnought race between Germany and Britain passed the Colonel quietly by as he devoted himself to all forms of sport and outdoor activities both in the Army and while on leave.

During 1904 and 1905, he was based at Crownhill near Plymouth where he frequently persuaded his brother officers to go bird-nesting. For the next two years, the Regiment was stationed in Gibraltar, although Campbell's involvement in sport often resulted in his being absent on special leave.

He did much of his bird-watching in Gibraltar with a local called José who was intrigued by his acquaintance's catapult which he used either to dislodge birds from their nests or to shoot one he could not identify. José asked to have a try, pulled the elastic but let go the fork instead of the sling, giving himself a black eye with a yell of 'Madre de Dios.' He did not try again.

During the winter of 1907/8 he was stationed in Bermuda and it was there that for the first time he met his future wife, May Brockman, whose father was a regular Colonel then serving in Bermuda. He married Miss Brockman in 1911. On 20th May 1908, he transferred to the Gordon Highlanders. Having fought beside the Gordon Highlanders in the Boer War he had come to admire them so much that it became his ambition to join them. Ronald Campbell maintained his interest in the Gordon Highlanders to the end of his life. As a 'Campbell' he had some initial difficulties in a Jacobite regiment, but soon became accepted for his own worth. He was promoted Captain on 22nd February 1909 and was said to have been the youngest Captain in the British Army, which was by now in the throes of a massive re-organisation under the direction of Viscount Haldane. Campbell's interest and participation in all forms of sport led to his appointment on 26th September 1910 as Superintendent of Gymnasia Southern Command, a post he held until the outbreak of the Great War.

He was Officer Middleweight Champion of the Army in 1905 and again in 1908 and, at the height of his form and at his weight, it was reckoned that there was no amateur or professional in the country to touch him. His chief trouble was that he was continually breaking small bones in his hands. He became a notable referee but was unable to get his views on boxing rules accepted outside the armed forces. He would stop a fight as soon as he felt that one boxer had developed a positive lead on points and before he could damage his opponent. The majority of officials objected that this ruled out the chance of the 'loser' landing a lucky knock-out.

Campbell experimented with ideas to take the brutality out of boxing throughout his long life. To this end he invented an air-filled boxing glove, while Director of Physical Education at the University of Edinburgh in the 1940's. He thought that this would make boxing faster and more skilful and at the same time minimise the shock of the blow and lessen the possibility of brain injury. The experimental glove was tried out by two of his stalwart assistants, Tom Houston and Major Charles Mather. 'Right,' said Mather after Tom had pulled on the glove, 'sock me on the jaw.' Tom, powerful and well built demurred. 'Go on,' insisted Mather, 'it won't hurt — just sock me on the jaw.' Tom hesitated for a moment and then let fly at the Major's chin. For a moment nothing happened. Then to Tom's horror the Major slid slowly to the floor and lay motionless. In the event, Campbell's theory had not worked in practice!

The air-filled glove had simply parted and Houston's partially unprotected knuckles smashed into the Major's chin, knocking him cold. After this unsuccessful effort Campbell took more interest in judo, which he felt provided many of the character-building features of boxing without its brutality.

As Superintendent of Gymnasia Southern Command, he operated from Command H.Q. at Salisbury. The new post involved widespread travel as his responsibilities covered all the counties from Hampshire to the west, south of the Thames. He was responsible for the standard of fitness training in his territory including the county regimental depots. He also promoted Games and Sports on a wide scale and encouraged individual units. As often as his duties permitted he was off bird-nesting with whichever officer he could drag along, and regular visits were paid to the Isle of Wight, Shawford (his wife's family home), Cosham near Portsmouth, and the Wyre and New Forests.

As Superintendent of Gymnasia he was regarded as something of a martinet. He thought it pointless to give notice of an inspection, as he liked to find out exactly how instruction was carried out in his absence. Slackers were given short shrift and one luckless instructor caught smoking on duty was immediately reduced to the ranks.

For a few years he drove round in a Ford which somehow or other he managed to buy and run on his army pay. On his own admission he was a terrifying driver as his mind was usually on 'higher things.' He never drove a car again after the Great War.

His intellectual awakening dates from this period. It was to flower twenty-five years later when Director of Physical Education at Edinburgh University.

During the Edwardian era there was an upsurge of scientific interest in the hidden forces which motivate human behaviour. Caught up in this exciting new movement Campbell began to read avidly, particularly the works of leading psychologists like Sigmund Freud who maintained that human action could be interpreted in terms of internal conflicts, sexual desires, and rebellion against authority. Disciples of Freud, such as Carl Jung developed new theories of their own and the debate was continued down the years by psychologists like Gordon Allport, who saw personality as a summation of traits such as honesty, scepticism and kindness. With his new awareness of the need for the scientific study of human behaviour, Campbell was now better able to examine those public school and army standards of conduct which so far he had admired, but taken for granted. 'To what extent,' he mused, 'are those standards of conduct inherited traits, and can they be inculcated by a scientific training?'

The interest was heightened when he was asked to comment on the draft manuscripts of Baden Powell's *Scouting for Boys* which was issued for comment in the early 1900's. Reading those documents forced him to think seriously about those attributes of character which were essential ingredients in the Chief Scout's philosophy. As time passed, he was better able to assess men and women, not only on the basis of his experience of life but also in terms of a growing intellectual maturity.

Meanwhile all was now set for an interesting but uneventful Army career followed by comfortable retiral on pension as an amateur naturalist in some country retreat. But the storm clouds were rapidly gathering over Europe. The holocaust of the Great War was just months away.

3

1914 - 1923

THE GREAT WAR

On 4th August 1914 Great Britain went to war against the Central Powers. The next day Captain Campbell rejoined the Gordons as Railway Transport Officer and shortly afterwards departed for France with the advance units of the British Expeditionary Force. The troop ships sailed up the Seine to Rouen where they arrived in the early morning to a great reception. The French greeted them with sirens blaring and bands playing. This was the first time that British troops had landed in France since Waterloo and Campbell did not miss his chance. He elbowed his way to the gangway. Before anyone could stop him, he sprinted down the gangway and on to the quay. Returning to his cheering comrades he claimed to be the first soldier of the B.E.F. to land in France. The B.E.F. pushed on into Belgium but it was impossible for the British and French armies to stem the German advance, and by the end of August the B.E.F. was in retreat from Mons. Conditions became chaotic and a paralysis of rail transport was only averted by the super-human efforts of the Railway Transport staff. They kept the railway organisation going by sheer improvisation, working day and night with occasional snatches of sleep.

By October Captain Campbell had re-joined his Regiment and was closely engaged in the heavy fighting. One incident reveals the un-orthodox streak that endeared him to his men and sometimes caused him to be regarded with suspicion by his superiors. His company was pinned down under heavy fire. They had suffered many casualties but stubbornly hung on to their positions. A message reached Campbell that the Guards had now moved up behind the Gordons — the Guards would die where they stood and the situation was secure. Campbell retorted in terms which dropped him — temporarily at least — to the bottom of the promotion lists. 'To hell with the Guards!' he growled. 'Cabbages die where they stand! If the Guards are any good get them up front and let the poor bloody Gordons out of here.'

While leading his company in action he was shot through the thigh near Lille on 12th October, 1914. The troops quickly rallied round their officer. 'I'm all right — move on,' ordered Campbell, realising the critical stage of the attack. 'We can't leave you here sir,' his men insisted. Campbell did not hesitate. His company was dangerously exposed.

'Sergeant,' he snapped, as he drew his revolver, 'take the men and get to hell out of here, or I'll blow your bloody brains out.' The sergeant hesitated for a moment, made Campbell as comfortable as he could, and then moved off with the rest of the company. Fortunately, relief was close at hand and Campbell was soon brought back to base hospital. The wound was serious enough to warrant a convalescent trip to England but did not cause permanent damage.

Once again he had brushed shoulders with fate. Even his doctor remarked that the bullet must have been guided by the hand of Providence. On his recovery he was retained at home. His services were urgently required to assist in the physical and bayonet training of troops in this country.

In the early days of the War the staff at Aldershot, including Campbell, had mostly rejoined their units as combatants. During the Battle of Mons, the High Command realised that this had been a mistake and set about re-establishing the Physical Training and Bayonet School at Aldershot. The job of recreating the Army Gymnastic Staff to cope with the volunteeers now flocking to enlist fell upon the newly appointed Inspector, Colonel Wright. Colonel Wright rapidly organised courses of physical and bayonet training for the new armies and those continued at Aldershot until the Armistice.

Training in bayonet fighting, a skill of which Campbell was the supreme exponent, became the responsibility of the School early in 1915. On 29th December 1914, he was re-appointed Superintendent of Gymnasia Southern Command. He was promoted to the rank of Major on 1st September, 1915, and on 27th October, appointed Assistant Inspector of Gymnasia.

Meanwhile in France, the Germans were trying desperately to break through the Allied lines. Although the British were forced back in November during the first battle of Ypres the line held and both sides settled down to the long ordeal of winter trench warfare. The position taken up by the rival armies in November 1914 remained substantially the same until the summer of 1918. The Allied line ran from the North Sea near Nieuport, along the Yser and bending just east of Ypres, crossed the Lys near Armentières and continued southwards west of Lille to the eastern suburbs of Arras, and thence by Albert on the Ancre to the Somme. A few miles to the south it bent eastwards to the Oise and thence along the Aisne and the Vesle to Reims. From there the trenches stretched to the borders of Lorraine and then bent southwards again almost to the Swiss border.

The British held the section from the Yser to near Arras and eventually took over more of the line until their posts extended to the Somme. For almost four years, constant engagements raged along the line and millions of men died without seeming purpose and with little gain either way.

James Cameron describes is as 'four long years of stalemate, of immobility of trench warfare, of wretchedness and indecisive death.'

The second Battle of Ypres during the late spring of 1915 threw great strain on the Allied Forces. In the Battle of Verdun (February - April 1916), the Germans were at last brought to a standstill — but at a vast sacrifice of life. The Western Front resembled a ghastly lunar landscape with regular and often continuous shellfire interspersed by suicidal advances against an invisible enemy securely dug in behind concrete trenches, pill boxes, and masses of heavily-spiked barbed wire. 'No Man's Land' lay between the opposing trenches sometimes only yards apart. It comprised a shell-pocked waste-land of desolation and death. When it rained heavily men, horses and guns sometimes disappeared without trace into the soft mud. Raiding parties operated in 'No Man's Land' and savage hand to hand encounters were fought out with knife, club, bomb and bayonet to the accompaniment of shell and mortar fire and the clatter of the machine gun. The slaughter on both sides reached terrifying proportions and an infantry officer's chances of survival were minimal.

Unlike the Second World War, however, the devastation was largely confined to the battle area. Elsewhere it was comparatively safe, and life tended to go on as usual in spite of conscription, which was introduced in 1916, and a shortage of supplies as a result of unrestricted German submarine warfare. There was a stark contrast between the comfort of the home front and the hellish conditions which existed in the trenches.

Veterans recall how they emerged as filthy lice-infected troglodytes from Waterloo Station, on leave from the Western Front, to be stared at by men and women in evening dress on route to the West End theatres. During those years while the Western Front was relatively stable, intense public interest centred on what was happening in the trenches, and places and individuals associated with the Front became household names. It was in this setting that Ronald Campbell became one of the popular heroes of the war.

THE 'BLOODY CAMPBELL'

By the autumn of 1915, the original professional Expeditionary Force had been virtually annihilated. But a new army of volunteers from all over Britain had swollen to more than a million men, grouped into three Armies with over forty divisions. Most of the new recruits were clerical and factory workers who had never dreamt of soldiering and yet they had to be forged into a mighty shield to protect the Western Front. The bloody battles of the Somme and Ancre lay in the months ahead and beyond that the long hideous wait until the arrival of the Americans. In the end of the day the issue would depend upon whether the Allies could hang on until American help arrived, and that in turn depended on the fitness and morale of battle-sickened troops.

By the beginning of 1916 the situation had become so critical that no one could foresee even a week ahead; days were the longest period in which to reckon. In an attempt to bolster up the situation the High Command decided to transfer some of its training units right up behind the lines. The time had at last come for Ronald Campbell to keep his appointment with destiny. On 2nd March 1916 he returned to France. This time there were no high spirits, no welcoming bands. He came quietly with a staff of fifty one instructors with the objective of establishing physical and bayonet training throughout the Western Front. He was the right man, in the right place, at exactly the right time.

Staff Instructors were sent to Etaples, Rouen and Le Havre while 31 went with Major Campbell to Flixecourt where they were absorbed into the First Army School of the British Expeditionary Force, at that time under the Command of Brigadier-General R.L. Kentish.

On the plateau adjoining the School at Flixecourt the first bayonet course for unit instructors was constructed and training started immediately. The first instructor at Flixecourt was Sergeant Major Terry.

'The Sergeant,' writes Siegfried Sassoon (*Memories of an Infanty Officer*) who visited the school and recorded some of his impressions, 'had been trained to such a pitch of frightfulness that at a moment's warning he could divest himself of all semblance of humanity. With rifle and bayonet he illustrated Campbell's ferocious aphorisms, including facial expression. When told to "put on the killing face" he did so, combining it with an ultra-vindictive attitude.'

General Allenby, then commanding the Third Army, was so impressed by the School that he asked for a special demonstration on the occasion of a visit by General Sir Douglas Haig and Sir John French. Sir Douglas Haig regarded the training of troops as being of paramount importance. Even old soldiers had to be taught new tricks and he particularly encouraged training in new methods. The French Commander who was also present remarked that the training was of great tactical value.

The Physical and Bayonet Training Headquarters eventually moved with the Third Army School to Auxi-lé-Château and it is not without significance that the Third Army, which was the first to appreciate the unique qualities of Campbell's training methods, was subsequently to make a magnificent stand against the German advance in 1918.

Major Campbell's staff had originally been sent to France for a two months' experimental period but their training methods proved so effective that they were directed to become part of the British Expeditionary Forces establishment. Headquarters were moved to a château at St Pol where they remained until bombed out in the German advance of 1918. St Pol lies some twenty miles north west of Arras and for four years was within long artillery range of the Western Front, although not actually shelled until March 1918. The château became Major Campbell's H.Q. and Officers' Mess. The assault course was almost a mile away and was laid out with systems of trenches, training equipment, bayonet fighting yards, obstacle courses and unarmed combat areas. Troops scaled walls, climbed and descended ropes and slides, leapt chasms and crawled along and under obstacles. One particular fiendish Campbell invention known as the 'bear pit' was situated beside the parade ground near the château. Outside it looked like an ordinary house with part of the roof missing. Inside it was dark and rigged up with booby traps for bullet and bayonet tests. The troops reckoned you went in like a lion and came out on a stretcher — lucky if you still had your trousers on!

Thousands of officers and N.C.O.'s destined to train the Armies on the Western Front attended this training depot during the course of the war. Troops were specially trained for trench raiding in which Campbell was an acknowledged expert.

Prior to a raid Campbell had the enemy trenches photographed. They were then reconstructed so that troops were familiar with the terrain before the attack began. He enthused the men to go 'all out' and roused them by quoting part of Henry V's speech before Agincourt. On the command they went forward like tigers.

Although now engaged in the training of troops rather than commanding them in the field, he was no depot-based officer. On the contrary, he had a hair-raising habit of going over the top when an offensive was on, carrying a periscope and accompanied by a terrified subordinate whose job it was to take notes. He was a man of tremendous courage. 'No Man's Land' held no terrors for him — or, if it did, he showed no sign of it. As a raid developed he methodically dictated notes in combat conditions. He and his instructors then worked out methods of dealing with situations which they had actually experienced. Crouched in a shell-hole he watched a Highlander kill a German by plunging his fork (which he happened to be carrying in his puttee) into the German's neck. His callous comment reflects the savagery of war. 'Can you think of a better weapon for killing a German waiter?' His nickname 'The Bloody Campbell' was well earned. He was well known to the Germans and included in the enemy black list for reprisals if ever he was taken prisoner.

Campbell reckoned that depot-based instructors were not suitable for the training of troops who had just returned from the line, and so the staff at St Pol took it in turns to go over the top with the raiders they had trained. They wore their distinctive instructor's uniform so that the troops would realise that their instructors were sharing the dangers with them. 'Leadership,' insisted Campbell, 'must be by example.'

By March 1917 the original complement of 51 instructors had risen to 10 Officers and 152 other ranks, of which 1 Officer and 16 other ranks were mentioned in Sir Douglas Haig's next despatches. A large number of Campbell's staff were scattered along the whole length of the Western battle front as lone individuals trying to keep troops fit and maintain morale.

Between May and August 1917 the Royal Engineers, assisted by German prisoners of war, built a large gymnasium at St Pol which helped the rapid expansion of the unit. The first monthly conference for Superintendents of Physical and Bayonet Training was held during December 1916 and continued until the end of the war. At this conference it was laid down that no money prizes would be permitted for any form of training in the B.E.F. In practice this rule was applied to boxing in 1917 and to athletics in 1918. The officers maintained that the men would only box for money prizes, and were surprised by the boxers who themselves generally preferred a medal.

During March 1918 the Germans launched their last great offensive of the War. They smashed through the thin line of the British Army between Sensee and Saint-Quentin and in a few days had pushed their advance to within a few miles of Amiens. Although the British stood firm at Arras the Germans further north nearly drove a wedge between the British in Flanders and their army in Artois.

On 21st March 1918, the German guns began to pump eleven inch shells into St Pol where Campbell's Training Headquarters had been established. As an emeny aircraft flew low overhead Campbell dashed out of the mess, grabbed a rifle, and loosed five rounds after it shouting, 'Of all the bloody cheek!' He was furious and got some instructors positioned under a hedge for a second run. To his disgust it never came.

The school and staff then formed into a battalion of two fighting companies (an event unique in its history) and remained an effective force until their dispersal on 4th April. Instructors were recalled to their headquarters from along the whole length of the front and on 24th March the Battalion under Major Huntingdon marched out of St Pol for Auxi-le-Château, the G.H.Q. of the Fifth Army.

The battalion paraded that day at the local Mairie. Parties were detailed for fatigues, road patrols, search parties for spies, every unattached soldier being challenged. Campbell commandeered a car, and with C.S.M.I.s Jimmy Driscoll and W. Wilcox as bodyguard, roared off eastwards to make contact with the enemy. It was rumoured that when G.H.Q. heard of the composition of the 'battalion' marching to its rescue they had hysterics.

C.S.M.I. Donald D. Lynch, for example, commanded a platoon comprising a Major, a Captain, two Lieutenants and 16 other ranks from sergeant to corporal. The battalion marched and counter-marched then dug themselves in behind Flixecourt but the battle did not come their way. On 28th March the German offensive suddenly swung south and was ultimately held by the British and French armies. The battalion then disbanded and on 5th April the School moved twelve kilometres north-west of Abbeville at Sailly-Bray and re-opened at Hardelot-Plage early in May.

On 11th October 1918, Campbell was appointed Inspector of Physical and Bayonet Training at Aldershot in place of Colonel Wright who had retired. Although pleased at Campbell's promotion the news was a great blow to all ranks of the Physical and Bayonet Training Staff in France. During his last months there was a flurry of activitiy at Hardelot-Plage which welcomed a series of official visitors including Military Attaches of the United States of America, Japan, Portugal, Serbia, Greece and Siam.

THE SPIRIT OF THE BAYONET

Colonel Campbell used the bayonet as a means of boosting the morale of war-weary troops. It was through his ferocity with the bayonet and his teaching of hand-to-hand combat that he became a legendary figure. One of the realistic features of his training methods was a demonstration between himself and his assistant, the boxer, Jimmy Driscoll, with naked bayonets. Both were actually wounded during some of the bouts. Up to 1914 the method of teaching bayonet fighting had been by means of a strong steel spring bayonet. This meant that the participants had to be heavily padded and protected by a strong mask. The new methods of teaching the bayonet devised by Colonel Campbell were used until bayonet fighting was discontinued. A former Army boxing champion himself, Colonel Campbell gathered around him well-known champions like Billy Wells, Jimmy Driscoll, Jimmy Wilde and Johnny Basham. Billy Wells had held the heavy-weight boxing title for nine years and by 1914 Jimmy Wilde had fought two hundred contests without being beaten. Jimmy Driscoll was an 'all time great' who subsequently published a number of books on the art of boxing. These men worked together in devising methods of unarmed defence against bayonet, knife, club, rifle butt and sword.

When a raiding party brought back from the German trenches a box of brand new spiked knuckle-dusters and maces, they were immediately sent to Campbell who used them on his instructors to find out the best methods of unarmed counter-attack.

In addition, the instructors taught the special uses of the Mills bomb and hand grenade in trench raiding. Colonel Campbell's highly special-ised training courses sent officers and N.C.O.'s back to their units with much more self-confidence in teaching others and capable of giving a good account of themselves in hand-to-hand fighting.

Like gladiators, Colonel Campbell and his instructors took on all comers, however heavily armed. The highlight was a fight between Driscoll and Wilcox. Sergeant Wilcox was reputed to have bayoneted eighteen Germans at the first Battle of Ypres when, in a frenzy of rage, he attacked a machine-gun crew who had cut down many of his pals. Colonel Campbell thought him one of the outstanding heroes of the war.

Spectators were awestruck at an unbelievably realistic battle between a world champion boxer and a real killer, and experienced troops some-times turned sick during the course of the demonstration. Campbell's enthusiasm for the real thing was somewhat dampened when one of his staff received a 'blighty' as a result of a bayonet attack. After that, contests were more carefully controlled.

This team of enthusiasts accompanied Campbell down the line where they gave demonstrations to troops under all conditions. Along the whole length of the Western Front they were affectionately known as 'Campbell's Travelling Circus.'

A rough circus they certainly were, and it is a tribute to the Colonel's tact and toughness that he was able to hold such a complex team together. Ex C.S.M.I. Donald D. Lynch vividly describes the Colonel in action. 'Campbell devoted one session to teaching unarmed troops how to fend off a bayonet. When the men were assembled in the gym, Major Campbell immaculately dressed, with Sam Browne belt, told the instruc-tor to have a go with the bayonet. The bayonet was not protected in any way and as the instructors were experienced veterans some would only do so half-heartedly. The Major's trick was to needle the instructor by cuffing him over the head. This caused the tormented fellow to lunge at Campbell, who parried the blade of the bayonet with his bare hand; whipped round; locked the instructor's arm and rifle under his armpit; detached the bayonet; and stabbed backwards at the instructor's stomach. All this was done with incredible skill and frightening realism.'

When it came to lecturing the Colonel was the star turn. Massive, sandy haired, with broken nose and battered ears, the Colonel pulled no punches as he worked the troops up into a frenzied hate against the enemy.

'The bullet and the bayonet are brother and sister — if you do not kill

him he will kill you. Stick him between the eyes, in the throat, in the chest — do not waste good steel — 6 inches are enough. What is the good of a foot of steel sticking out of a man's neck. 3 inches will do for him — when he coughs, go and look for another — kill them! Kill them! There is only one good Bosch and that is a dead one.'
(Siegfried Sassoon. *Memories of an Infantry Officer.*)

Such homicidal eloquence and crude jokes inspired Siegfried Sassoon to write his well-known poem on the bayonet entitled 'The Kiss.'

To thee I turn, in thee I trust
 Brother lead and Sister steel
To his blind power I make appeal
 I guard her beauty, clean her rust.

Sweet Sister, grant your soldier this
 That in good fury he may feel
The body where he sets his heel
 Quail from your downward darting kiss.

According to Robert Graves, Siegfried Sassoon varied between happy warrior and bitter pacifist. The poem was originally written seriously but later he offered it as a satire; the poem succeeds whichever way it is read. Robert Graves and Siegfried Sassoon attended the first courses at Flixecourt in 1916 and were profoundly impressed by the Colonel's performances which were discussed in Army circles for years afterwards.

Colonel A.W. Brocks served with Colonel Campbell on the Western Front and was, until he retired, Director of Physical Training at Aberdeen University. 'It is impossible,' says Colonel Brocks, 'to express in words the dynamic impact of Ronnie Campbell's talks to troops in the field. He would address troops — sometimes a Brigade strong — in the open air, and stimulate their fighting spirit to a remarkable degree. His talks to the troops contributed more to the fighting morale of the Army in the First World War than he has ever been given credit for.'

Lieutenant General Sir Gifford Martel also pays tribute to Colonel Campbell's work in his memoirs. He writes that he 'sometimes wonders if any other individual did as much to raise morale in the troops during the Great War.' General Martel was a Staff Officer at the Headquarters of the Tank Corps in France during the second half of the war.

He recalls in his memoirs that a talk by 'Ronnie' Campbell to the troops did more to restore their fighting spirit than several weeks in rest billets, and that there were few people who served on the Western Front who did not know him. He was as well known to Dominion troops as to the Imperial Forces. When conditions were really bad and the troops felt they had had enough, Campbell had the uncanny knack of suddenly appearing out of nowhere. His morale-boosting talks, usually delivered from an army wagon tailboard, were famous for their ruthless anecdotes. Killing was the name of the game. 'When a German holds up his hands and says: "Kamarad — I have a wife and seven children." What do you do? — Why,' said the Colonel, 'You stick him in the gut and tell him he won't have any more!'

He played a particularly vital part in sustaining the troops after the March retreat of 1918 when morale was at a desperately low ebb and American help seemed a long time in coming. Perhaps the greatest tribute of all is expressed by one of his staff:

'Campbell's psychological understanding of men was phenomenal. His appearance in the devastated areas was like a visit from God.'

When Australian and Scottish troops mutinied at Etaples and made open war on the Military Police, Colonel Campbell sent in his staff with sports gear and the dissident troops gradually laid aside their arms for boxing gloves and footballs. Campbell undoubtedly made one of the greatest personal contributions to the ultimate success of the allies on the Western Front where he was as well known as any of the great national military commanders.

Between 1915 and 1917 the celebrated French author, André Maurois, while serving on the Western Front, found time to write *The Silence of Colonel Bramble* and *The Discourses of Doctor O'Grady*, two of the enduring humourous masterpieces to have come out of the First World War. One has little difficulty in identifying the fictitious Commander of the Gamaches training camp so vividly described in the *Discourses*.

'Major Macleod a blood thirsty Scot whose hobby was bayonet work. Major Macleod, however, was original in one respect he favoured verbal suggestion rather than actual practice for the manufacture of his soldiers. For the somewhat repulsive slaughter of bayonet fighting, he found it necessary to inspire men with a fierce hatred of the enemy. "Blood is flowing" he used to repeat as the training proceeded and the Highlanders drove their bayonets in the bags of straw shaped like German soldiers. "Blood is flowing and you must rejoice at the sight of it. Don't get tender-hearted, just think about stabbing in the right place. To withdraw the bayonet from the corpse, place your foot on the stomach." I was really curious to hear him, relates the fictitious character, Doctor O'Grady, because people at G.H.Q. were always talking about the extraordinary influence he had over the troops morale. "One of Macleod's speeches," said the Chief of Staff, "does the Huns as much harm as ten batteries of heavy howitzers." '

Doctor O'Grady recounts the story of Private Briggs by whom our Major Macleod seems to have been caught out — a shy refined little fellow, who sold neck-ties in peace time. He loathed war, shells, blood and danger. Poor Briggs, he lands up with Dr O'Grady at Gamaches and sits through a lecture by Macleod on the Spirit of the Bayonet.

'The lecture began,' recounts O'Grady 'with a ghastly description of the shooting of prisoners and went on to a nauseating account of the effect of gas, and a terrible story about the crucifixion of a Canadian sergeant, and then, when our flesh was creeping and our throats dry, came a really eloquent hymn of hate, ending with an appeal to the avenging bayonet.

'Macleod was silent for a few minutes,' continues O'Grady 'enjoying the sights of our haggard faces; then convinced we were sufficiently worked up, he went on, "Now, if there is anyone of you who wants anything explained, let him speak up, I'm ready to answer any questions." Out of the silence came the still small voice of Private Briggs. "Yes, my man," said Major Macleod kindly. "Please Sir, can you tell me how I can transfer to the Army Service Corps." '

Hypnotic powers of public persuasion is a gift enjoyed by many great political and religious leaders and Colonel Campbell was well aware that such a gift could be used either for evil purposes or to achieve great good. 'If only Hitler had been motivated by the lofty idealism of St Paul,' he remarked, 'the destiny of Europe could have been altered for the benefit of mankind.'

Although Campbell's renown on the Western Front was closely identified with his prowess with the bayonet, he took it all with a 'pinch of salt.' He reckoned that his enthusiasm for the weapon was sometimes misconstrued by his contemporaries, many of whom thought that he regarded it as a practical weapon.

'To be truthful,' he later confided, 'it was all a bit of ballyhoo. Even by 1914 the bayonet was obsolete. The number of men killed by the bayonet on the Western Front was very small, but it was superb as a morale booster. Get the bayonet into the hands of despondent troops and you can make them tigers within hours. I found nothing better to introduce recruits to the terrible conditions which awaited the poor devils up the line.'

REHABILITATION TRAINING

Among Campbell's other major achievements at this time was the introduction of rehabilitation training into the Convalescent Depots in France. Recreational training was introduced into the Depots by the Physical Training Staff long before it was officially sanctioned. Eventually it received the enthusiastic support of the Adjutant General and was carried out until the Armistice. In January 1917, the King's Physician wrote to the Physical Training Staff that they would feel flattered if they could see the wonderful results achieved in Convalescent

Depots by physical and recreative training.

In the early days of the First World War there was not the same appreciation of battle fatigue as there is today. Men who broke down under shell fire were regarded as cowards and were sometimes executed. Campbell recognised that a man could only stand a certain amount of battle strain and so he provided special depots for shell-shocked soldiers. These Depots were designed to achieve conditions of tranquility. One of these consisted of a farm at Hardelot-plage where soldiers could recuperate in pastoral conditions. Shell-shocked soldiers were dressed in smocks and encouraged to work the land and tend and rear animals. Off duty they played games and indulged in all kinds of physical pursuits.

One badly shell-shocked soldier did not respond to Campbell's treatment. He sat morosely alone — lost in a world of unreality. Campbell tried his best to awaken some spark of interest, but without success. The Medical Officer wanted him moved to a psychiatric hospital in England but Campbell pressed for more time. 'I can cure this man,' he insisted, 'there must be some way to get through to him. Get him into a psychiatric ward and he may never come out.' 'A hopeless case,' replied the Medical Officer, 'but I give you two weeks — we cannot keep him here any longer.'

The days went by but still Campbell was unable to restore the man to normality. 'What are his hobbies?' he asked but none of the other patients knew anything of his previous history. Came the last day and Campbell seemed to have failed. Desperately he again questioned the other patients. At last came the information he was seeking; 'If it is of any help sir,' volunteered another soldier, 'I once heard him talking to himself about roller canaries.' That was the Colonel's opening. He sat down beside the shell-shocked soldier and remarked, 'I have been trying to breed roller canaries for years but have been most unsuccessful. I hear that you are an expert — can you help?' For a moment there was a silence, then a glimmer of interest came into the other man's eyes. Falteringly he began to tell Campbell about roller canaries. The conversation continued and for weeks the pair discussed how to get the best results from breeding roller canaries. But one day the conversation widened and soon the soldier was cured and, within a few months, had returned to the Western Front.

Campbell's work with convalescents is best described by Sir Phillip Gibbs in *The Realities of War*.

'Colonel Ronald Campbell retired from bayonet instruction and devoted his genius, and his heart (which was bigger than the point of a bayonet) to the physical instruction of the Army and the recuperation of battle-worn men. I liked him better in that job, and saw the real imagination of the man at work and his amazing self-taught knowledge of psychology. When men came down from the trenches, dazed, sullen, stupid, dismal, broken, he set to work to build up their vitality again, to get them interested in life again, and to make them keen and alert. As they have been de-humanised by war, so he rehumanised them by natural means. He had a farm with flowers and vegetables, pigs, poultry and queer beasts. A tame boar named Flanagan was the comic character of the camp. Colonel Campbell found a thousand qualities of character in this animal, and brought laughter back to the gloomy boys by his description of them. He had names for many of his pets — the game cocks and mother hens; and he taught the men to know each one, and to rear chicks and tend flowers and grow vegetables. Love, and not hate, was now his gospel. All his training was done by games. Simple games arousing intelligence, leading up to elaborate games demanding skill of hand and eye. He challenged the whole Army system of discipline imposed by authority by a new system of self-discipline based upon interest and instinct. His results were startling, and men who had been dumb, blear-eyed, dejected, shell-shocked wrecks of life were changed quite quickly into bright cheery fellows, with laughter in their eyes.'

Colonel Campbell achieved a large measure of success with his technique, the principles of which are now universally recognised as sound psychological medicine. Yet he was not happy. 'It's a pity,' he said, 'they have to go off again and be shot to pieces. I cure them only to be killed — but that's not my fault — it is the fault of the war.'

In spite of his immense prestige on the Western Front, Ronald Campbell was certainly not happy. To understand his outlook at that time, as well as his subsequent career, it is necessary to go back to that fateful meeting at the Orange River some fourteen years earlier when the Royal Canadians remained in comparative safety and the Gordon Highlanders moved up to join Lord Methuen at the Modder River. Lord Methuen commanded the Kimberley Relief Column. Having defeated the Boers at the Modder River, he intended to strike northwards towards Kimberley but the way was barred by a Boer Army under General Cronje. The Boers were strongly entrenched along a low hill known as Magersfontein. They had dug themselves in along a front of almost three miles and their trenches were protected by a mass of barbed wire entanglements. Lord Methuen decided to take the position by a night march followed by a dawn assault. The Highland Brigade commanded by Major General A.J. (Andy) Wauchope was selected to lead the attack. The Brigade consisted of the Seaforths, the H.L.I., the Black Watch and the Argyle and Sutherland Highlanders. The Gordons, arriving from the Orange River, were held in reserve.

On 9th December Lord Methuen opened with a great bombardment, the effect of which was mostly dissipated in empty trenches. The night march had begun at 12.30 am and as the Highlanders began to deploy in the early light they came under a withering fire from the Boer trenches packed with skilled riflemen. The Highlanders went down in their hundreds. Rushing towards the Boer trenches they impaled themselves on the barbed wire till they were 'strung out like crows.' There was little cover. The best a man could do was to lie flat and hope for the best. Still Lord Methuen kept up the attack.

At midday the Gordons were ordered forward. Charging through the battered remnants of the Highland Brigade the Gordons in turn were crucified on the wire and mowed down by the deadly rifle fire. With their stricken comrades they had to hang on as best they could under a boiling South African sun. Lord Methuen battled on but by dusk the troops were so shattered that the attack was called off and a truce arranged.

The British lost nearly 1,000 killed, wounded and missing, of whom 700 were Highlanders. Five Highland Battalions lost their Commanding Officers. For days afterwards, the postman, like an angel of death, went round the farms and villages of Scotland delivering War Office telegrams. Overnight, the nineteenth century techniques of European armies had become obsolete and the way had been prepared for the static warfare of the Western Front. Bitter controversy subsequently raged over Lord Methuen's tactics at Magersfontein. 'Andy,' Wauchope is reputed to have said, 'This is madness!' as he led the Brigade forward. If he did not say these words others certainly thought them. Many of the Highlanders believed that they had been sent to certain death.

Colonel Campbell was not at Magersfontein but afterwards he fought alongside the Gordons and became a Gordon Highlander in 1908. He was however present at Paardeberg when, after ten days of heavy fighting, the Royal Canadians led the final assault. After Kimberley had been relieved a strong force of retreating Boers had skilfully dug themselves in, along a stretch of the Modder River near Paardeberg Drift. Lord Roberts had suddenly been taken ill and, on 18th February 1900, Kitchener, who had assumed command, decided to overwhelm the enemy laager by a series of frontal assaults. Troops hurled themselves at the enemy throughout the morning but were cut down by the entrenched Boers. The brunt of the fighting was borne by the Highland Brigade and the Mounted Infantry under their commanding officer, Colonel Hannay. Confusion reigned among the various units engaged and General Smith-Dorrien who commanded the 19th Brigade, which included the Royal Canadians, records that during most of the time he was in a 'complete fog.'

The day wore on with nothing to show for it but mounting losses which sickened the older officers. Although the troops were at the end of their tether, Kitchener ordered Colonel Hannay once again to rush the laager at all costs. At three o'clock Hannay made his own ultimate gesture. Sending his staff away on various pretexts he spurred on his horse and charged alone into the Boer positions. So determined was his attack that the Boers had no choice, and he fell riddled with bullets inside the Boer lines. His grave is there today beside the Modder River where he lies with so many of his comrades.

Like Lord Methuen at Magersfontein, Kitchener still kept up the attack, and hopeless bayonet charges continued against the Boer positions until nightfall. There were 1300 casualties that day — a repetition of Magersfontein. Colonel Hannay's sacrifice, however, was not in vain. Shattered by the slaughter — Kitchener's commanders demurred, and the following day appealed to the more humane Lord Roberts, who came from his sick bed to take over personal command of the operations.

The lessons of Magersfontein and Paardeberg had been largely forgotten by the British High Command by the time of the Great War, and infantry were frequently sent in against heavily fortified entrenchments with inadequate support. As a result there was an unnecessary sacrifice of life from which Europe has not yet recovered.

General Haig, essentially a cavalry man, and his immediate staff, remained remote from the battlefields on the Western Front and never really understood the appalling conditions in which infantrymen fought and died. Nor was there sufficient consideration given to the technical means by which the defensive conditions could be overcome.

Ronald Campbell never forgot the lessons of Magersfontein and Paardeberg. Unlike most of the High Command he actually went over the top with the raiders he had trained and had first hand experience of life in the trenches. He was an infantryman by training and instinct. He was no Kitchener, determined to secure military objectives regardless of the cost of human life. Although he had the fighting spirit of Hector Macdonald he also had the compassion of Lord Roberts as well as the inventive ingenuity of Baden Powell. His blood-curdling exhortations were part of an act which was very necessary for its purpose. Underneath he was a sensitive and humane man who would never knowingly have sent infantrymen forward into certain death. But the same fate which was to raise him from the ranks to a top job at Aldershot dealt him a cruel backhanded blow. His destiny was to train men. Although he played a vital part in maintaining morale on the Western Front at a critical period of the war he was neither to command men in battle after 1914 nor to direct overall strategy. He was a specialist in physical training and bayonet fighting and his immense popularity was due to charismatic qualities of leadership rather than to his official position in the hierarchy of command.

Against the massive scale of operations on the Western Front he stands alongside such nationally known individuals as 'Woodbine Willie' and Tubby Clayton of Toc H, rather than the military commanders. His agony was to be a lynch-pin in a system of warfare which he must have found utterly repugnant. As a professional soldier he had to do a distasteful job to the best of his ability. As the war unfolded he became increasingly aware that the issue would ultimately depend on which side could maintain its morale in a ghastly process of attrition over which he had no control. His duty was clear — he had to see it through.

He was unhappy, but in his unhappiness he was already thinking of a better world beyond the war, and coming into contact with men who were equally troubled and who in their time would share their idealism with him and give up much to create a better Britain. Out of the holocaust there came the urge to rebuild.

For his services during the first World War, Colonel Campbell was given a Brevet, awarded the D.S.O., mentioned three times in despatches, and gained five foreign decorations. The American Distinguished Service Medal, the Belgian Order of the Crown, the Legion of Honour, the Portuguese Order of Avis, and the Siamese Order of the White Elephant. The Siamese Order of the White Elephant was awarded for advising the Government of Siam in regard to physical training. The Portuguese decoration was won for organising a reprisal raid in rather unusual circumstances. Some Germans had captured a party of Portuguese and cut the seats from their trousers, applying bright green paint to what was exposed. They then let their prisoners return to their own lines with a discourteous message about their zoological gardens being already filled. The counter-raid for which Colonel Campbell then trained the Portuguese was carried out with a fury and valour which completely restored their morale.

He was appointed Superintendent of Gymnasia G.H.Q. British Armies in France on 2nd March, 1916, Deputy Inspector of Physical and Bayonet Training G.H.Q. British Armies in France on 21st May, 1917 and Inspector of Physical and Bayonet Training at Aldershot in 1918. He held the latter post until 1924. He was promoted Brevet Lieutenant Colonel on 3rd June, 1917, temporary Colonel on 11th November 1918 and finally Colonel on 3rd June, 1921.

'WOODBINE WILLIE'

While at the Fourth Army Infantry School in France, Colonel Campbell 'discovered' G.A. Studdert-Kennedy, well-known to a former generation as 'Woodbine Willie,' a nickname given by the troops because of the unlimited supply of Woodbine cigarettes which he gave away on his

34

rounds. This outspoken padre had come into conflict with the establishment who had sent him to the Infantry School in France to get him out of
the way. Colonel Campbell was impressed with Kennedy and invited him
to speak at one of the church services in St Pol. Owing to an attack of
asthma he could not take the service but he spoke at a smoking concert
that evening which was open to civilians as well as soldiers. Kennedy
came on to the stage smoking a cigarette and commenced with the
remark: 'I know what you're thinking — here comes a bloody parson.'
The startled audience were soon held spellbound by his magnetic
personality, and Kennedy was immediately accepted by the men as one of
themselves.

Colonel Campbell subsequently appointed Kennedy as his chaplain.
Typically he made the condition that there would be no compulsory
parades and that if men could not be attracted voluntarily the padre
would get 'the sack.' The Colonel made no mistake about his man. In
spite of the fact that there were no compulsory parades, the area around
the church-hut continually swarmed with men trying to attend 'Woodbine
Willie's' services. Some would lie listening on the roof, while others stuck
their heads through open windows. 'Never once,' said Campbell, 'did he
fail to hold their attention and inspire them with the big things in life. He
was a man with a wonderful insight into character and I never met one
who was more firm. He would box anybody, he would ride any horse and
he would face any general who attempted to criticise his methods.'

Kennedy subsequently joined Campbell's 'travelling circus' of which
the boxer, Jimmy Driscoll, and other well known athletes including the
subsequent film star Victor MacLaglan were members. Although
asthmatic, Kennedy would spar with Jimmy Driscoll and give demonstrations of unarmed combat. These 'circuses' were part of Campbell's
morale boosting techniques which he later expanded and developed in
civilian life. The 'Assaults at Arms' which took place in the McEwan
Hall in Edinburgh between the wars were a civilian development of those
earlier war-time shows.

TOC H

About the same time as Campbell set up his headquarters in St Pol, an
event took place some 35 miles north in an obscure Flemish town called
Poperinghe which in time was to weave another strand into his extraordinary career. During 1916, in this first habitable town west of Ypres,
the Reverend P.B. Clayton, familiarly known as 'Tubby Clayton,'
opened a rest house for soldiers. The Club was known as 'Talbot House'
soon shortened in signaller's language to 'Toc H.' Part of the house was
used as a chapel — a carpenter's bench serving as a communion table or

altar. The rest house with its camaraderie became known throughout the trenches and, like 'Woodbine Willie,' 'Tubby Clayton' soon joined the host of colourful characters associated with the Western Front.

After the war men who had served in the trenches wanted something in civilian life to take the place of Talbot House and at a meeting in London during 1919 Toc H was founded. Branches were formed throughout the country and in 1922 the movement was incorporated by Royal Charter.

Every member of Toc H is pledged to undertake voluntary service such as hospital visiting, the care of incapacitated, or work among youth. 'Tubby' Clayton himself was closely connected with the work of the London Federation of Boys Clubs.

Colonel Campbell knew 'Tubby' Clayton on the Western Front and became one of his close friends. In the early days 'Tubby' depended to a great extent on the Colonel's help and encouragement. After the war the Colonel was caught up in the enthusiasm of the movement and it was largely as a result of his influence that Toc H places such emphasis on voluntary service.

NO SMOKING

Early in his army career, Colonel Campbell realised that the habit of smoking tobacco was damaging both physically and morally. Originally a heavy smoker, he gave up the habit after the Boer War and during the rest of his life was a convinced non-smoker. He was particularly scathing in his comments on the leader of youth who was unable to do a job unless he had 'a fag in his mouth.' Colonel Campbell was responsible for an army investigation into the effects of smoking on bodily health and in particular into the condition known as 'disordered action of the heart.' The survey was carried out by a team of doctors of whom half were smokers and half non-smokers. The enquiry established that the non-smoking soldier had a much better health and fitness record than the soldier who smoked. As a result smoking was banned in the army while men were on duty.

Unfortunately it has not been possible to document these particular facts with absolute certainty as Colonel Campbell was a modest man who seldom took personal credit for his enterprising ideas. Much however is to be found in the records of the Royal Army Medical College. During the period 1908 - 1918 when Campbell was having an increasing influence on physical fitness in the Army there was considerable interest by commanders in the habit of smoking.

The Commanding Officer of the 1st Seaforth Highlanders campaigned against smoking prior to 1911. At the same time, Lt. General Sir L. J. Oliphant, G.O.C., Northern Command, issued orders prohibiting excessive cigarette smoking by young soldiers serving under him, and directed medical officers detecting cases of injury to health produced by cigarette smoking to draw the matter to the attention of Commanding Officers.

Field Marshall Lord Grenfell was also struck by the harm that the increasing prevalence of cigarette smoking appeared to be doing to the health of the Army, and alluded to it in General Orders as not alone a military question but one of national importance. In order to help men overcome the habit the Field Marshall prohibited smoking when men were on fatigues or under arms, including field operations and manoeuvres.

On 2nd February 1917, a National Health Insurance Medical Research Committee published a report on 'Soldiers returned as cases of "disordered action of the heart" (DAH) or "valvular disease of the heart" (VDH)' which contains reference to the effect on cigarette smoking by patients in the Survey. The Army must have been at least forty years ahead of its time in appreciating the health hazards of cigarette smoking and there is little doubt that the Colonel had a considerable influence on the enlightened views of the Commanding Officers concerned. He hated the habit which he regarded as damaging not only to health but to morale. He also saw it as an offence against the Scottish virtue of thrift.

NO STAMPING

Another of Colonel Campbell's ventures was to try and stop the army habit of 'stamping.' While watching the Guards going over an assault course he came to the conclusion that the repeated hammering of the metal-heeled army boot, either on guard duty or in jumping, resulted in minor concussion, with the result that the soldiers could become confused and therefore less responsive to commands. Colonel Campbell condemned the practice on every possible occasion and in 1923 had a large notice posted in every gymnasium, including the Guards, to the effect that stamping was prohibited. 'If a soldier has to stamp,' he growled, 'he should do something constructive, like stamping on a spade.' Colonel Campbell actually took his theories on 'stamping' a good deal further and maintained that soldiers would march better if army boots had no heels and for a time he tried to persuade the army authorities to issue a standard boot of soft leather designed to give a good fit, but without a heel. He recalled with a twinkle in his eye that this was one battle with authority that he never had a hope of winning. Although unable to convince the Army to do away with heels, he had lasts made to his own requirements and wore bespoke footwear manufactured without heels. With the now widespread adoption of the rubber heel and of plastic soled commando-type boots, the problem is probably not so acute now as it was when Colonel Campbell served in the Regular Army.

AMATEUR SPORTSMANSHIP

Colonel Campbell continued his interest in boxing during the post Great War period. He had been a leading spirit in founding the Navy and Army Boxing Association in 1911 and after the 1914-18 War was largely instrumental in having the Services turned over from professional to amateur boxing. General Martel records that it seems almost unbelievable that there should have been any difficulty in the Services in turning from professionalism. Yet the difficulty was very real. It would no doubt have been possible to obtain some official ruling that professionalism should cease but, says General Martel, 'Little advantage would have been gained from such a ruling, and that was not Campbell's way of running an Association. A willing consent from every unit was his goal.'

During his service at the Army Inspectorate, Colonel Campbell staged 'black and white' demonstrations which were immensely popular at the time and did much to raise the standard of refereeing and judging in the Services and in amateur boxing circles. The Colonel's elder son, Bruce, witnessed some of these contests and recalls that as a small boy he was present at a number of demonstrations:

'The idea, like many of Pa's, was brilliantly simple: one boxer in white strip was virtuous and aggrieved; his opponent in black committed foul after foul, with a pause between each, while Pa explained what had happened and what to look out for. The demonstration had to be carefully rehearsed and while many good boxing instructors played the two parts, one Black stands out: Sgt. I. Mills, an Army champion at one of the lighter weights. Saturninely handsome and with a rich black moustache, he was made for the part and executed his fouls with diabolical relish amid roars of laughter.'

Colonel Campbell consistently advocated amateurism in sport. His reasons were philosophical and reflected his basic contention that the development of the body was closely associated with the growth of the mind and the spirit — in other words, with the enlargement of the character of the whole person. In Colonel Campbell's book there was certainly a place for the professional — but it was a limited one. For example, he preferred to choose his staff from the ranks of those whom he used to call 'gifted amateurs' rather than from those who had made physical training their profession from college days.

In his opinion, the function of the professional was to teach rather than to perform, and the essential qualities of the true professional were ability, and love of the game coupled with a flair for teaching others. It is also important that the teacher set a good example in his personal life. He disliked professional football which was then in its infancy, and commented then that if men were paid to play football, in fifty years they would be 'bought and sold like cattle.' Throughout his life he had little regard for organised football, other than in friendly and amateur matches.

With strange perversity, however, he took a keen interest in professional all-in wrestling, possibly because some of the better known contestants had been members of his Western Front team. When at Edinburgh University, he sometimes invited lady members of the staff to the bouts which were then held in the 'Eldorado.' It amused him to see their reaction to the violence, which he regarded as magnificent showmanship. On occasions, those old pals were invited to give demonstrations in the gymn where they taught the students some of the more bloodcurdling techniques.

Apart from his interest in professional all-in wrestling, the Colonel espoused amateurism in the Olympic and other international games with which he was closely associated after the First World War. He resigned from committees on which he served when it was decided to appeal for large sums of money particularly from industry, in order to meet the expenses of a national team. The Colonel considered this to be wrong. Amateurs came together as best they could and competed together with whatever facilities were available or not. What mattered was the spirit in which the contestants met — not the resources behind them, nor the results.

It must not be inferred, however, that he did not encourage high standards. This he certainly did, but the standards were to be obtained by sheer hard work in spare time, with the use of existing facilities and not at the expense of work, studies or one's obligations to contribute to the general well being of the community. Colonel Campbell gave no encouragement to the athlete who devoted years of his life, to the exclusion of everything else, to the winning of a medal in a particular international event. 'That is an activity for a performing animal,' he would chuckle, 'not for a man.'

Colonel Campbell was in no way worried at the difficulty this country might experience in international contests if his policy of true part-time amateurism were adopted. He believed that Britain must set her own standards in sport and make it clear to other countries that she will only compete with them on that basis. He was convinced that many nations would willingly respond to such an invitation and the outcome could only be an increase in international goodwill and understanding. Those countries who wished to pursue quasi-professional or more specialised standards in sport, should be left to go it alone. 'If this course were adopted,' he said, 'the standards and values of this country must eventually dominate the world of international sport.'

In terms of the XXth Olympiad of 1972 in Munich, Colonel Campbell's philosophy of sportsmanship runs counter to much current thinking in modern athletics. Although the 1970 Commonwealth Games in Edinburgh seemed to bring out the best in the participants, national obsession with the collection of medals and the breaking of records dominated the subsequent Olympics. The Scottish Olympic runner, Ian McCafferty, who failed to gain a medal in the 5000 metres, summed up this attitude: 'I reached for the top prize and failed. Nothing less could satisfy me now.'

Gunter Grass, a leading post-war German writer commented in similar vein that he was impressed by the contrast between the gaiety of the public and 'the grim, almost obsessional determination of the competitors who were set on achieving high records.' It was John Rafferty, however, writing in the Scotsman, who crystallises a view which in recent years has been gaining increasing support:

'It was shocking how few in swimming and track and field produced a personal best. The trouble is that we have been lulled for too long with British standards and have not matched ourselves against world standards.

'Some, such as Bedford and McCafferty, and Jenkins and Stewart, did break away and aimed high and if they did come unstuck reaching for gold then their failure must be treated with charity. It is the great mob who celebrate being third in a heat who must be looked at and pruned. The United States won 91 medals and it would have done the British Olympic Committee good had they listened to the recriminations over such failure and the blasting of the administration and the coaching. It might have pushed ambition into that long standing attitude that it is nice to be there and jolly good if we get into a final.'

Earlier in the same article he slams the happy-go-lucky attitude of the British women's contingent:-

'The girls particularly disappointed, and even when watching them walk about the village it was clear they would win nothing. They looked like a lot of wee lassies going to school sports. The magnificent East German girls looked the part — and indeed there are very few great athletes who do not.'

As long as Colonel Campbell is remembered his ideals and inspiration will stand as an uncompromising challenge to this kind of thinking. Were Colonel Campbell alive today he would quietly encourage the 'wee lassies' at their school sports and the 'thirds' in the heat mob, and leave John Rafferty to blast the British Olympics Committee to his heart's satisfaction and go his own way with the magnificent girls from the German Democratic Republic.

Colonel Campbell had no regrets at not winning an Olympic Medal. He was gratified at having fought his way through to the semi-final of the Olympic Sabre Pool and relished his encounter with the great sabreurs of his day. What mattered to him was the lofty ideal behind the action, the thrill of the encounter, and the lasting friendships made through participation in the Games. Medals and records were but tokens of a transient success. All honour to those who achieved the ultimate success but the real glory was in participation, not in victory.

Colonel Campbell was the great post Great War exponent of the British standards of good sportsmanship now so often decried, and between the wars his views profoundly influenced World and European sport. His ideals were particularly well received in the Netherlands and, by invitation of the Anglo-Dutch Society, and with the permission of the War Office, he toured Holland and lectured on British games and sportsmanship. The effectiveness of his work is aptly illustrated by the following incident recounted by Major Mather who became the Colonel's chief instructor at Edinburgh University. During a gym session, scepticism was expressed at Campbell's ideas of sportsmanship and a student commented that in practice they would not work. Major Mather overheard the remark and turned brusquely on the speaker: 'Don't underestimate the Colonel!' he said.

'I was once sceptical but I have seen him in action. He has done far more for British Sportsmanship than he has been given credit for. I was with him at an international fencing competition in Brussels during the early 20's. The competitors were mostly continental — and there were the British; standing up like gentlemen, acknowledging their hits while the continental boys were getting away with murder. One bout made me absolutely sick. The British competitor had clearly won the contest, but lost because his Belgian opponent failed to acknowledge several very good hits by the Britisher which were missed by the judges. I was disgusted and going outside found myself beside the Belgian team who were congratulating the winner. There they were jabbering away, pleased as blazes — while I wanted to clobber the lot of them. "Cor blimey!" The next moment the Belgian captain appeared out of nowhere. He was in a blazing temper and marched straight up to the winner and told him that his win was a disgrace. My French is not all that good but there is no doubt what the Belgian captain was getting at. The team just stood there with their mouths open as their captain pitched into them. In his opinion the contest should have gone to the British. "You can do what you like with the other competitors," he said, "but the British are different — they are real sportsmen. The next time you fight the British it doesn't matter a damn if you lose — but you will acknowledge your hits." '

That simple story conveys a profound message to all those who are engaged today in any form of competitive sport. Colonel Campbell's conception of sportsmanship stands as a challenge to much of the competitive nationalism and obsessional dedication to excellency which today characterises so many major athletic events.

ALDERSHOT

The Physical Training Headquarters at Aldershot which Colonel Campbell took over during the Autumn of 1918 was largely the creation of three outstanding soldiers, General Horace Smith-Dorrien, Colonel the Honorable John Scott Napier and Lt. Colonel Sir Malcolm Fox.

When General Smith-Dorrien came to Government House in 1907 as G.O.C. he greatly improved and increased the playing field provision as well as doing much to enhance the general well-being of the soldier. He also introduced cross country running. The swimming pool is a lasting memorial to Colonel Napier who was appointed Inspector of Gymnasia in 1897. Colonel Napier built the pool without official support and largely financed the building with funds obtained from Assaults at Arms and the Royal Military Tournament. Hundreds of thousands of troops have taken their first swimming lesson in the pool which was opened in 1900. Colonel Campbell devised his own technique for the systematic teaching of soldiers to swim.

But the father of the Physical Training Headquarters at Aldershot was Colonel Sir Malcolm Fox who was Inspector of Gymnasia from 1890 to 1897. A schoolboy athlete, Colonel Fox served in the 100th Canadian Regiment, known as the Leinster Regiment and later in the 42nd Highlanders. He took part in the Egyptian Campaigns and was severely wounded at Tel-el-Kebir in 1887. He was appointed Inspector during 1890.

It is not inappropriate that the portraits of Colonel Fox and Colonel Campbell — two robust Highlanders — should gaze down together from the walls of the Officers' Mess at the Army Training School. Colonel Campbell was a schoolboy when Colonel Fox was at the peak of his army career and if the two ever met they were certainly not on familiar terms. But Colonel Fox was a big man and cast a long shadow. His influence was to be seen everywhere in Army Physical Training and consciously or unconsciously Colonel Campbell was affected by the work of his great predecessor, which in turn he adapted, rationalized and improved.

By coincidence, Colonel Fox may unwittingly have sparked off a train of events which resulted in Colonel Campbell succeeding him in office a quarter of a century later. His keenness for boxing was such that he managed to introduce the art of boxing into many of the English Public Schools. On 30th March 1894, the first Public School Boxing and Fencing Championships were held in the presence of Colonel Fox in the gymnasium at Aldershot. Among the lads taking part in the boxing section was young Ronald Campbell. To Colonel Fox, therefore, Colonel Campbell owed his first introduction not only to boxing — a sport in which he was to excel — but also to the Fox Gymnasium which is at the very heart of the Army School of Physical Training.

One of the first tasks of Colonel Fox was to introduce athletics into the Army and it was due to his determination that in the early 1890's a new headquarters gymnasium was built at Aldershot and an Army athletic ground laid out on waste ground. When the War Office objected to the cost, Colonel Fox paid the bill himself. He also introduced boxing into the Army, but this was just the beginning.

He found in Army Gymnasia up and down the country much weird and expensive apparatus with instructors whose conception of proficiency was the ability to perform all sorts of tricks on it. Colonel Fox reckoned this was all right for a circus but not for army training. Following upon an extensive European tour he was impressed by the work of the Royal Centre Gymnastic Institute at Stockholm and as a result the Swedish method of physical culture was introduced for the first time into the Army gymnasia. He improved the standard of Army swordmanship by bringing Italian experts to England as instructors. Colonel Fox initiated bayonet fighting competitions in battalions and companies as well as at the Royal Naval and Military Tournaments. He invented the spring bayonet for training purposes and devised a series of simple rules for the training of soldiers.

After leaving the Army, he was appointed Inspector of Physical Training to the Board of Education in England — a post he held between 1900 and 1910. By the time he retired, a scheme for the physical training of children was in operation throughout the whole of England. Colonel Fox died on 23rd March 1918 — just seven months before Colonel Campbell was appointed Inspector. He had, however, laid the foundations on which Colonel Campbell was to build his own unique contribution to the science of physical training; in boxing, fencing, athletics, bayonet fighting and physical training for all — without the use of elaborate apparatus.

In 1918 the Army School of Physical Training at Aldershot comprised the Fox Gymnasium, the Swimming Baths and the Command playing field, together with some training areas. In the early 1920's a football pitch with cinder track round it and grandstand was built alongside the Fox gym. There was no residential accommodation and the Inspector and his staff lived in 'digs' locally. Administrative and messing accommodation were also minimal. Nonetheless those spartan surroundings had seen the training of countless thousands of troops during the previous four years. During the 1914/18 war the Gymnasium was covered in ivy and troops exercised so close to the building that they could watch the birds hatching their eggs. As the season wore on, the fledglings matured and flew off to a life of their own.

Just as Colonel Wright's task in 1914 had been to build up the Physical Training Staff to meet the urgent demands of the Great War, so Colonel Campbell had just as difficult a job pruning the staff and organising the school to meet peace-time requirements. Contraction was rapid. On 11th November, 1918 the strength of the school was 2,299. In 1919 the number was reduced to 200 and by 1922 the staff numbered 150 as the Army returned to a peace-time footing. Instructors' certificates were introduced in 1919 and soon the school had over 400 students on simultaneous courses. Many of those taking Certificate courses were staff instructors who were re-qualifying. The Certificate issued by the School enabled Army instructors to obtain P.T. appointments in civilian life. Following the tradition of Colonel Fox, Colonel Campbell introduced courses in Boxing and Fencing and engaged a maître d'armes to teach the staff to fence. He also kept up the interest in agriculture which he had so successfully developed at the convalescent farm at Hardelotplage. At Aldershot he created a small holding comprising allotments, chicken runs and pigeon lofts. It continued to function effectively until the mid 1930's.

HIS INFLUENCE ON POST WAR PHYSICAL TRAINING

As Inspector of Gymnasia (later changed to Inspector of Physical Training) Colonel Campbell was responsible for the standards of fitness of British troops throughout the world, and for the efficiency and distribution of instructors as well as for administration everywhere. The post involved wide and constant travel by boat and train. The responsibilities of the Inspector are virtually the same today although he now mainly moves about by air.

During his Inspectorship, Colonel Campbell introduced into Army physical training ideas and methods evolved during the war, which made it vital and purposeful. He was particularly keen on games which developed the team spirit and boosted morale. During the War he had encouraged the playing of games behind the lines, particularly football, and witnessed for himself the therapeutic value of free play on men who were at breaking point. He never left a unit without ensuring that regimental competitions were instituted in all forms of athletics and games. He went so far as to have silver cups and trophies sent out from Britain for rear area dispersion. Sometimes his games were almost childish like 'tig' or 'leapfrog' but they were organised with competitive teams. Campbell intuitively knew that the British soldier does not like to be beaten — even at 'tig.' He continually refined his 'games' techniques and he reduced them to a fine art in his later University days. In all this he exercised a powerful influence on the development of physical education in post war Britain. Peter C. McIntosh's authoritative study, *Physical Education in England since 1800* aptly assesses the work of the Army Gymnastics Staff during the first World War in its historical perspective:

'the reasons for the broadening of the official conception of physical education were numerous. The effect of new ideas and practices abroad was considerable. The chief cause of the increased emphasis on games and outdoor activities was correctly diagnosed by the Chief Medical Officer when he wrote in 1917: 'The work of the Army Gymnastic Staff in England and France during the War will undoubtedly have far-reaching results on the recreative side of physical training for children and adolescents as well as soldiers. The playing of games in a comprehensive and organised way for their mental and physical effect has never before been fully attempted as part of any scheme of physical training.

'The overwhelming success which has attended the general intro-duction of games behind the lines in France suggests that we have made far too little use of our national aptitude and love for games in the education and training of the young man and as a means of whole-some recreation for the adult.'

A contemporary reference to Colonel Campbell's influence on post Great War physical training in Britain is to be found in an article by Captain Frank Starr appearing in *The Army Physical Training Journal* of 1924. This illustrates the national importance which was placed on Campbell's work by his contemporaries:-

'Denmark has Nils Bukh and village clubs, and Nils Bukh's pupils have put pep into the village clubs. Britain has not a Nils Bukh, but it has a Colonel Ronald Campbell, who, as Inspector of Physical and Games Training during the war put pep into an army far bigger from first to last than Denmark's entire population. What is more, before he retired from the Service, the Inspector of Physical Training set afoot a movement which can do as much for the hamlets of England as the doctrines of Nils Bukh have done for the villages of Denmark. All who have heard Colonel Campbell's lectures — it would be hard to find a soldier-man who had not — will agree that as morale developers they will take some beating, and probably will agree that the teaching of his instructors was almost a tonic. With the Armistice the Physical Training Inspector began to organise for peace, as he had organised for war. When his staff was reduced to peace establishment, he set to work deliberately to fit his instructors to play their part in country life when, time-expired, they retired on pension.'

Colonel Campbell also originated a scheme of tests for use as a yardstick to measure progress and keep the training on practical lines. He was always on the lookout for new ideas and invited outside lecturers to deal with such subjects as 'The Art of Teaching,' 'Youth Care,' 'Social Rehabilitation' and 'Alcohol and Smoking.' Among the speakers was Professor Frank J. Adkins, a most unmilitary figure, who held the Chair of Education at one of the London Colleges. During a discussion the Professor commented that 'The remarkable thing about Colonel Campbell is that he has worked it all out from first principles.' He was also keen on visual aids and sported slogans in large letters in prominent places around the gymnasium at Aldershot. One of these was painted over the main door of the Fox Gymnasium at Aldershot and bore the legend: 'Seest thou a man wise in his own conceit? There is more hope of a fool than of him.' Everyone attending a course at Aldershot had to stand and read this notice before he could enter the gym.

Colonel Campbell was an organiser of exceptional ability and did much to rationalise the teaching of physical training in both military and civilian circles. He urged the adoption of universal terminology and standardisation of equipment and many of those ideas were gradually adopted during the next two decades.

He was greatly aided in his work by the wide experience he had gained by his inspections of systems and study of methods of physical training in other countries. These included visits to centres in the Princeton and Pennsylvania Universities and to West Point Military Academy. In Europe, he visited centres in Brussels, Utrecht, Amsterdam, Copenhagen, Lund, The Sokol in Prague and the French Army Physical Training School at Joinville. The Sokol was founded in 1862 by Miroslav Tyrs and Henry Fugher both of whom sacrificed the best years of their lives and the greater part of their incomes to the welfare of the cause they created. It became the most powerful gymnastic organisation Czechoslovakia. At the end of 1923, it had 645,000 members.

The French Army School employed the Herbert system concentrating on natural movement for running, jumping, lifting and scaling. He also visited Nils Bukh's School at Ollerup in Denmark. Nils Bukh's methods were in many respects controversial, particularly his stretching exercises, but they had a profound effect on men's gymnastics both in Denmark and in Britain and greatly influenced Army Physical Training, particularly after 1927.

THE ROYAL TOURNAMENT

The Royal Tournament is now a popular television spectacular. The first Military Tournament and Assault at Arms was held from 21st to 26th June, 1880 and, achieving Royal Patronage, it became the Royal Tournament. These Tournaments were highly dramatic presentations of Army life and skills. They were noisy affairs with continuous movement of men and horses, the banging of drums and the rattle of musketry. The rousing finale with a standard implanted by the assaulting troops to the tune of "Rule Britannia' received enthusiastic cheering. In 1914, its twenty fifth successive year, the Tournament ceased for the duration of the Great War. However, only a month after the Armistice, the Organising Committee was summoned to meet and Colonel Campbell was appointed a member. The first post-war Tournament on 26th June, 1919 had as one of its features a demonstration by the Army School of Physical Training of P.T. as it was carried out in the field during the War in France. In subsequent years, the Army School mounted contests using weapons such as rapier and dagger, broad sword and buckler. Quarter staff encounters were another source of lively entertainment.

Colonel Campbell took a keen interest in the Tournament and assisted in its organisation even after his retiral. He organised the fencing and bayonet fighting competitions which went on during the mornings of the Tournament and had in addition the unique distinction of competing. Not only did he win the Officer's Sabre Competition in the last pre-war Tournament in 1914 but he won the Officer's Bayonet Competition in 1919 and the Army Bayonet Championship two years later.

His genius, however, was in the organisation of dramatic finales, usually with a Scottish flavour. The first of those involved the story of the Fiery Cross. Later he presented the Battle of Killiecrankie and also some of the events of the '45.

On one occasion, a hundred pipers were on parade and the massed Scottish troops danced several 32some reels. The Colonel's suggestion of the 32some reels was originally greeted with scepticism by the purists but in the end the reels were impeccably worked out by an authority on Highland dancing. Although the Colonel had little interest in the theatre he was a natural actor with a dramatic flair. This latent talent was encourage by some of his friends including the comedian Seymour Hicks and the film star Victor McLaglan.

NO SABBATICALS

Stories about Colonel Campbell's service years are legend and undoubtedly he was one of the officers who inspired the imagination of Andre Maurois when writing the exploits of the celebrated Colonel Bramble and *The Discourses of Doctor O'Grady*. The character of Colonel Bramble was indeed based on a number of Colonels whom the author encountered on the Western Front, but it is doubtful if those included Colonel Campbell who was a Major at this time. As mentioned earlier, however, the character of Major McLeod in the *Discourses* fits the Colonel like a glove.

An Army pensioner, Mr J.T.P. Ashe, tells the following story which he regards as typical. In 1919, Ashe was contesting the welter-weight division of the Army Boxing Championships at Aldershot:

'Shortly before the contest we welter-weights were summoned to the office. To our surprise we were greeted by Colonel Campbell who was seated there with Major 'Mick' Leahy. I knew Mick well as he had been an army heavy-weight boxing champion before the war. His boxing days were over, or so I thought — as he had lost a leg at Mons. "Well boys," said the Colonel, "Mick here has promised his old girl that he will bring home one more silver cup before he hangs up his gloves for good. With one leg left at Mons he will just make welter-weight if he screws off his new one before he weighs in." There was a stunned silence. Only Colonel Campbell could have thought up that one. He just sat there looking at us with that quiet smile of his. "It will not be too bad! he said, "If old Mick finds it hard going he'll just screw off his leg and crack you over the head with it. By jove! — that will bring the chaps to their feet." The ice was broken and we laughed half-heartedly. "All right, give it a try," we said, half hoping that Major Leahy would think better of it. To my dismay I was drawn against Mick in the first round. What a show! The crowd cheered their heads off and any misgivings I had were soon dispelled as Mick clobbered the daylights out of me. As it was, I just managed to struggle home on points.

'No one, except Colonel Campbell, could have suggested that a one-legged heavy-weight box welter-weight and get away with it. The local papers went to town and for once I was a celebrity.'

On a visit to an Army base at Bermuda, the Colonel found the morale of the garrison at a low ebb. 'The troops are fed up and need to play games.' he suggested to the Commanding Officer. 'There are no playing fields here and the sooner we get one built the better.' 'Where?' replied the C.O. 'Every time I go for a bit of ground it seems to be needed by the War Office.' 'In that case,' retorted Campbell 'we will make our own land. By jove — look at that hill. It's serving no purpose. Let's get the lads to throw it into the sea. It will make an excellent base for a playing field and there can be no complaints by the War Office or anyone else.' And so the troops started to it. Bucket by bucket, week in, week out. Eventually the job was done and a playing field built on land reclaimed from the sea. It is still in use.

In the Officers' Mess in Gibraltar, a discussion arose about how far a white man could run on foot in tropical conditions. Most of the officers assumed that only Africans acclimatised to the heat could run in the tropics for any length of time. 'Bosh!' interjected the Colonel, 'if a fit man of any country plans his day he can easily cover fifty miles.' This remark was greeted with derision. 'All right,' he retorted, 'you are all on! I'll run fifty miles tomorrow.' Early next morning he started off and performed the incredible feat of running fifty miles before dusk. His batman made a fortune out of the episode by advising that the Colonel would never complete the distance and at the same time laying his own bets quietly on his officer.

While on active service he found himself extremely irritable during the evenings. Thinking the matter over he pinned a postscript to his next letter home: 'P.S. Please send on a pair of slippers.' His comrades laughed when they arrived, but not for long. Their worth was quickly appreciated and soon every officer had a pair.

The Colonel's methods were not always appreciated, and he had a reputation as a disciplinarian. He insisted that troops under his command had to carry out normal duties even when involved in other activities. This sometimes caused irritation, as most Commanders allowed footballers and other athletes special privileges, being excused normal fatigues.

Not so with the Colonel: if extra jobs had to be done he expected his men to rise earlier, re-organise their time, work harder, and more efficiently. At Edinburgh University he told students that it was not enough to study and pass examinations. As potential leaders they had the capacity to play a worth while part in the life of the University. In addition he encouraged them to get involved in community work outside the University. This was extremely successful. According to records kept by the Pollock Gym staff the Colonel's students achieved better academic results than the average for the whole University. 'My job,' explained the Colonel, 'is to enlarge a man's capacity so that he can cope effectively with several activities at one time without fatigue. I try to ensure that when students leave the University they are not just physically fit. In boxing terms I want them to have the intellectual dexterity of the lightweight, supported by the moral punch of the heavyweight. When the heat is on my boys will come out on top.' There were no sabbaticals in the Colonel's scheme of life.

4

1923 - 1929

THE BOYS' CLUB MOVEMENT

When his appointment as Inspector of Physical Training ended in 1923, Colonel Campbell was offered the command of a brigade. Eight years earlier he would have jumped at the chance but now he was looking to wider horizons. He decided instead to resign from the Army and accept an appointment as Honorary Treasurer to the London Federation of Boys' Clubs. His immediate reason for entering the Boys Club movement was the encouragement he received from Mr W. McG. Eagar, one of the founders of the National Association of Boys Clubs, and for many years Honorary Editor of *The Boy*. Eagar wrote the final form of *The Principles & Aims of the Boys Club Movement* and was the author of *Making Men* — an authoritative history of the Boys Club movement in Great Britain. Eagar himself had a remarkable career and when he retired in 1949 *The Times* did him the singular honour of devoting a leading article to his work for the blind. At one time the Assistant Director of the Borstal and Central Associations, he was subsequently appointed as Inspector of the London Housing Board. From the outset Colonel Campbell was inspired by the kind of men whom he found dedicating their lives to the Boys Club movement in post-war Britain. Three men in particular made a profound impression upon him: Father S.B. Rawlinson, a Roman Catholic; Basil Henriques, a Jew; and the Reverend James Butterworth, a non-conformist.

Father Rawlinson, a distinguished Army Chaplain, along with Francis Geoghegan, a London accountant, had aroused the interest of the Roman Catholic Church in the Boys Club movement as early as 1907. Basil Henriques and his wife not only ran the famous Jewish Club, The Bernhard Baron Settlement at Stepney but lived at the premises. He was one of the oustanding Boys Club leaders of his day and was a J.P. on the Juvenile Court sitting at Toynbee Hall. James Butterworth, an unconventional Methodist Minister and a former Great War combatant, devoted much of his life to a London Club in derelict Walworth Road not far from another famous Club in Hollington Street.

Colonel Campbell felt that a movement which could bring such remarkable men together for a common purpose and also transcend religious differences was the place for him. The roots of Colonel Campbell's association with the Boys Club movement, and in particular with the London Federation, went very much deeper however than the encouragement he received during 1923. Once again he seems to have been caught up in a march of men and events. In 1897 an Oxford graduate, Dr John Stansfeld, had started a medical mission in Bermondsey in East London. The local people were mainly dockers and tannery workers. Conditions were appalling and crime was part of local everyday life. Policemen would only patrol certain streets in pairs and some they would not enter at all. Medical services were virtually non-existent. In 1900 one W.C. and one stand pipe had to serve twenty-five houses. Even so, the water was turned on for only two hours each day but never on Sundays.

Dr Stansfeld's work inspired others. Soon he was joined by Oxford graduates prepared to work in the district on a voluntary basis. Out of this movement there sprang a number of Boys Clubs and by the outbreak of the Great War four clubs loosely linked together were clustered round the dockland district. These were the Gordon, Dockland, Decima and Canterbury Clubs. The clubs, although separate, worked together and stimulated enthusiasm by engaging in every possible competitive sport.

Prior to the Great War men, later to be closely associated with Colonel Campbell were connected with those clubs. Tubby Clayton who founded the Toc H movement and Sir Alexander Paterson, later His Majesty's Prison Commissioner, were two such men whom Colonel Campbell had met in France. Paterson took a special interest in difficult boys and promoted many measures to reform their treatment in Borstal.

After the war, as the survivors returned to the dockland clubs, many of the leaders had a four-fold contact through the Army, Borstal, Toc H and the Boys Club Movement. They were a dedicated band of brothers with exceptional ability. It was only natural, therefore, that on retiral from the Army, Colonel Campbell should gravitate towards dockland in London's East End and start working with men whom he knew, in whose aspirations he shared, and where the need was greatest.

When Colonel Campbell threw in his lot with the Boys Club movement he was at the zenith of his Army career. His future was assured and there is little doubt that such an outstanding officer with all the right contacts would have achieved the highest honours. He deliberately left a comfortable public life for a life of comparative obscurity among the deprived youth of East London. From being a living legend he quietly disappeared into the Boys Club movement.

With characteristic thoroughness Colonel Campbell went to live near dockland among the lads whom he wanted to help. Living 'all in' at ten shillings a week he identified himself with the local community. For a time he had 'digs' in Trinity Square, Southwark, and found an old Music Hall Jingle very apt to his condition —

At Trinity Church I met my doom
Now I live in a top back room
Told me her age was Five & Twenty
Cash in the bank — of course she'd plenty
I like a fool believed it all
I was an M U G.

Trinity Square, south of London Bridge, was within walking distance of the dockland Clubs. It was an area where many Boys Club volunteers lodged. Conditions there were so bad that during part of the time he was working in London his wife lived in the family home away from the city.

Those were the years of the General Strike and the depression. Colonel Campbell witnessed scenes of poverty and degradation that haunted him to the end of his days. The social conditions of East London in the twenties had more resemblance to the worst features of the London of Charles Dickens than the London of the 70's. Children died of starvation. Men wore their boots out looking for work. Poverty stared the majority in the face and housing conditions defied description.

While working in dockland, Colonel Campbell taught and organised physical training, boxing, fencing and all kinds of activities in the four clubs. He got to know the people and was a familiar figure in the district. He was particularly associated with the Gordon Club which was situated underneath the Lucas Tooth Gymnasium in Tooley Street. The building was demolished in 1973.

After the second World War, the four Bermondsey clubs found that they were unable to continue and they gradually closed down. There were several reasons for this. Improved conditions in the district; lack of funds and the shortage of leaders; and better provision of youth facilities by the local authority. Fortunately, however, the work has not all gone, and a new club called the 'Canterbury, Oxford & Bermondsey Boys Club' has been opened in Page's Walk, not far from the area served by the original four clubs. The old boys of the former dockland clubs have also opened another well-attended club called the 'Stansfeld'. This caters for former members of all the clubs, past and present. There is little now left to remind us of the Bermondsey clubland of Colonel Campbell's day but his spirit must surely live on in the little gym with its boxing ring on the first floor of the Stansfield Club and in the dedication of the Boys Club leader, Reg Hopkins.

Colonel Campbell also lived and worked in Bedford House — a Boys Club run by his old school. At that time the Club was located at 9 Sandland Street, some two and a half miles across the river in Holborn. In 1928 the Club moved to new premises in nearby Lamb's Conduit Street. Both premises were destroyed during the last War. New clubrooms were subsequently rebuilt but the club has now been discontinued as there is not the same need in the district.

When Colonel Campbell first came to Bedford House the gymnasium was under-used. The club leaders naturally expected that the gym would be the chief scene of Colonel Campbell's activities and were disappointed to find him ignoring the gym and sitting in the canteen chatting with the boys, playing draughts and telling his inimitable jokes. They had, however, misunderstood a fundamental demonstration of the art of leadership. Colonel Campbell had to get to know and understand the boys before he could lead them. It was not enough to breeze in, take an activity, and then head home.

The resident club men at Bedford House lived very simply. The Warden, Scoutmaster and Club Leader, M.G. Lightfoot, lived on the club premises so that they could open up immediately after they came home from work. Each resident had a small bedroom, and there was a common room. A conscientious caretaker and his wife took care of their simple needs.

The club leaders, who were part time unpaid volunteers, returned from their normal work about 6.30 pm and after a quick cup of tea, opened the club to the boys at 7. They did this every evening and kept the club open until 10.30. It was not until 11 o'clock at night that they sat down to their evening meal. This was also the hour when the leaders visited one another.

It was in this self-sacrificial way that the Boys Club movement advanced after the First World War. Then, voluntary youth work demanded personal commitment for many nights a week over a number of years. Perhaps there is now a tendency to underestimate the amount of attention which young people require and the value of dedicated voluntary commitment. Whenever the Colonel stayed in the Bedford Club, he was up with the others well into the morning hours, sharing experiences and his fund of stories. Later, when visiting London in connection with formal functions, he made a point of spending at least part of his evenings with the Bedford Club men. The Colonel soon became a familiar figure in Holborn and Bermondsey where he would be found in the streets at almost all hours of the day and night.

In the autumn and the winter months, London still boasted the roast chestnut and roast potato men with their braziers glowing on hand barrows. These were mostly ex-servicemen and Colonel Campbell made it his business to know each one of them by name. In the cold night air he warmed himself at the barrows and bought potatoes or chestnuts and chatted while he ate. He was idolised by the men. They were eager to talk to him, and not only about their troubles. They shared their jokes with him as well. Such was the esteem in which he was held that none of the veterans tried to trade on his sympathy but simply discussed their problems with him honestly and openly. Even talking to the Colonel seemed to boost their morale. In many instances, however, he found a way to give practical help. As one of his surviving friends of that period puts it — 'His vibrant character and pulsating goodness left an indelible impression on all those with whom he came in contact.'

One of the Bedford leaders at that time was Geoffrey Martin who has many happy recollections of those far-off Boys Club days. He will never forget the Colonel's friendly, unconventional, humorous and loveable personality. One day Geoffrey was walking down Regent Street with Campbell who was well dressed, and bowler-hatted as befitted a retired Army Officer. Spotting one of the Club boys on a tradesman's bicycle, the Colonel put two fingers to his mouth and unconventionally attracted his young friend's attention with a piercing whistle. After grinning and waving each continued on his own way.

Another memory is cherished by Geoffrey Martin. Colonel Campbell would enter the common room late in the evening when the leaders had just sat down to supper, clad only in his pyjama trousers. 'He would stand with his back to the fire vibrating his cheeks, arms and torso to the accompaniment of apelike noises all intended to tone up the body and make for health.' He had studied the habits of those animals and learned to imitate them while serving in South Africa. Sometimes when the onlookers were finding this impromptu performance hilarious the house-keeper would enter to clear away the remains of the supper only to make an immediate exit. Even in later University years, he would delight his friends with his amazing imitation of a lively baboon. When his audience was completely captivated, he completed the act by mimicking a chameleon which had flicked its tongue at a fly on a fly-paper, got its tongue stuck, and then had a fearful struggle to get his tongue free.

Colonel Lelean who had soldiered with the Colonel through the Boer War narrates that in London:

'Isolated from most of his old friends, and conditions which had made his life in the army so pleasant, Colonel Campbell gained an intimate knowledge of the life and conditions of the slums which matched the knowledge of nature which he had acquired by intense study of the birds and other animals inhabiting the remote wilds.'

Colonel Campbell was so moved by the terrible conditions that for a time he became radical in outlook and considered resigning from the United Services Club. On Lt. Colonel Garnier's advice, he did not do so and eventually found it of great therapeutic value to relax occasionally in the comfortable quiet of the Club away from the drab surroundings of East London. Colonel Garnier of the Royal Marines was for many years Chief Instructor at the Lucas Tooth Gymnasium where voluntary leaders were trained for club work.

The Lucas Tooth Institute was founded in 1913 when Sir Robert Lucas Tooth gave £50,000 to start a Boys' Training Fund. In 1925 a new gymnasium was opened in an old school in Tooley Street, and courses were held from then onwards to qualify young men to become instructors of physical training in boys' clubs and other youth organisations.

Colonel Campbell recounted endless stories of his work in the East End and had an unexpected gift of reciting Cockney poems. One of his 'hardy annuals' unfolded as follows:- Two cockneys were hard at it in the boxing ring. By the end of the second round one of them had his nose flattened as well as two half-closed badly blackened eyes. As his second was on the point of throwing in the towel, a wag shouted from the back of the hall: 'It's orl right 'Arry, 'it 'im from memory.'

One of his most poignant stories concerned a boy boxer whom he found sobbing his heart out after taking a beating. 'Son,' said the Colonel, 'it's not as bad as that — after all a good loser shouldn't show his feelings.' 'It's not that, sir,' replied the boy, 'but I've only had a bag of peanuts all day. With a full belly I would have knocked his block off.'

Later at student work camps, he would have the company chanting the cockney refrain: 'Wot no muvver? Wot no farver? Pore child.' This was a cockney ritual invented by cockney regiments to overcome their lack of brass or pipe bands — or so Colonel Campbell said. While in London, Colonel Campbell must have lived like a cockney, thought like a cockney and talked like a cockney. On occasions he recited long extracts from Kipling. He was much inspired by the poet's literary works, although he felt the man himself lacked warmth.

One of Colonel Campbell's first acts on joining the staff of the London Federation of Boys' Clubs was the introduction of a 'Federate' scheme to enlist the support of a large number of 'Federates' who would undertake a small annual subscription to the Federation. A Federate gave a minimum of five shillings and undertook to enrol others. A Federate became an 'Associate' on enrolling twelve new members and a 'Fellow' on enrolling thirty. The highest award was 'Companion' for those who enrolled sixty new members. Colonel Campbell was one of three 'Companions.'

Colonel Campbell also introduced fencing into the Boys' Club movement. There was much opposition to this at the time. Long serving leaders felt that it was a waste of time to teach 'East End kids' how to fence; but to Colonel Campbell fencing was more than a game. Through fencing he taught a way of life; of generalship and of playing the game. 'Why do you kiss the hilt of your sabre before a contest?' he would ask the beginner. 'Because the hilt of a sword was originally shaped in the form of a cross. To kiss the cross means that you intend to conduct the bout in a spirit of chivalry. Your opponent then knows that you will fight like a gentleman and acknowledge hits against you — even if they are not seen by the judges or the referee.'

Many a youngster had his life completely changed by being introduced to the art of fencing and to the high standards of personal conduct which the Colonel demanded from those who took part in the sport.

Colonel Campbell quickly realised that the boys preferred the sabre to the foil. He cut out the tedious learning of stances and strokes, and let them fight naturally as they learned. In a few months he had a team which could compete with highly trained fencers of Bedford School. Men of distinction at Salle Bertrand found that the club boys could give them a good fight. One young man named E. Liebe reached the final pool in the Amateur Sabre Championships.

While working in London Colonel Campbell paid scant attention to his own material needs and his wife had to bring up the family on a tight budget. In order to make ends meet part of the Colonel's army pension had to be commuted.

It was while Colonel Campbell was in London that he wrote his first book, much of it when on holiday in Salen, Argyle. This was a collection of vivid boxing stories published in 1926 entitled *A Ten Round Contest*. The stories are all based on actual events most of which took place in Clubland. The book was subsequently re-issued as: *The Spirit of the Fist*. He later published a novel: *The Foster Brothers*. The story had a North Argyll setting and he used his children and his friends as characters. He was also the author of a number of text books on his system of physical training.

Colonel Campbell's last literary effort was to start a history of the Edinburgh University Athletic Club. It was his own idea and he undertook much of the research before his hip and eye operations in the 1950's. The work was almost completely rewritten by his great friend Colonel Charles Usher, who succeeded him at Edinburgh University as Director of Physical Education and subsequently published as *The Story of the Edinburgh University Athletic Club*.

The work of the London Clubs never ceased to interest Colonel Campbell. He wrote regularly to the Federation and it was only because of his partial blindness during the last three years of his life that his wife wrote on his behalf.

Colonel Campbell was present at a weekend conference at Toynbee Hall from 23rd to 24th October 1923 when it was decided to form the National Association of Boys' Clubs. On that occasion he was one of the principal speakers and put forward a scheme of physical training based on exercises which could be carried out in confined spaces without special equipment and by boy leaders instead of instructors. His theory was that training should be based on games and aimed at creating all round efficiency. The formal decision to found the National Association was taken at a conference held during October 1924 at Coleshill, Birmingham. the National Association was taken at a conference held during October 1924 at Coleshill, Birmingham.

Colonel Campbell was appointed Honorary Treasurer of the London Federation in 1923 and served in that office until 1927.

He was a member of the Executive Committee of the National Association from its formation in 1925 until 1930. In 1928 he resigned from the London Federation to become Joint Secretary of the National Association with Colonel L.F. Ellis. Colonel Campbell held the post as Joint Secretary until 1930. Thereafter, he was a Vice President of the National Association from 1930 until 1940.

GOOD AND VALID

Once the National Association of Boys' Clubs had been formed it became obvious that a unified statement of faith and purpose was required. The problem was formidable; the strands which had to be woven together were immensely varied as boys' clubs had been formed throughout the country with different objectives.

The Manchester Lads' Club, for example, sought to prevent the fierce gang warfare which was then raging in the city streets. Elsewhere the purposes were evangelical or educational. Some clubs operated as a social service in areas of poverty and neglect. By 1930, however, an agreed philosophy had been hammered out and in that year the Annual Conference accepted a document entitled: 'Principles and Aims of the Boys' Club Movement' as a statement of faith and purpose.

'The Principles and Aims' was the work of W. McG. Eagar assisted by Colonel Campbell, Basil Henriques and L. F. Ellis. While the finished document was a composite effort, the Colonel's influence shines through in the importance which was placed on all-round physical, mental and spiritual fitness.

It is not an abstract statement based on psychology or social science, but represents the distilled wisdom of hundreds of club leaders expressed through the genius of four outstanding authors.

Although the mid-Victorian roots of the Boys Club movement were much older than the Boys' Brigade founded in Glasgow by William Alexander Smith in 1883, or the Boys Scouts launched by Baden-Powell in 1907, the club movement had neither the simple Christian objective of the Brigade nor the precise moral and patriotic purposes of the Scouts.

The acceptance of the Principles and Aims at the Annual Conference of 1930 was thus deeply significant for the movement as a whole. Frequently referred to as 'the N.A.B.C. Bible' it gave the movement a new unity of purpose as well as clearly defined and distinctive methods.

In the introduction the authors enunciate their primary purpose. 'The NABC has ... to show why a National Association has been formed and what practical results it hopes to achieve. It has, in fact, to produce a programme, a policy and a philosophy; a programme of what is to be done, a policy of how to do it, and a philosophy in answer to the most important question of all — Why are you doing anything, and why form clubs to do it.'

With its emphasis on fitness for citizenship, manhood, and work, the Principles and Aims is a document which clearly reflects the high moral approach of the authors to the work of the movement.

The place of religion is defined under the general heading of 'Fitness.' In contrast to the evangelism of the Boys Brigade and the practical approach of Baden-Powell the Principles and Aims envisage a club as 'not treating its members fairly if it fails to recognise their spiritual needs. Whatever its religious atmosphere or background may be, it must teach that man's mind and spirit dwell in his body and that man — and we should say God — must be served in the beauty of that Holiness which is wholeness, that is the harmonious development of all a man's faculties. The boy instinctively reverences Truth and Justice and Love. The club must help him to identify these with Him who is their source.'

In assessing Colonel Campbell's influence on the Boys' Club movement, and in particular his part in formulating the Principles and Aims of the National Association, one cannot do better than to quote the following passages from W. McG. Eagar's history of the Boys' Club movement *Making Men*:-

'The acceptance of the Principles and Aims of the Boys' Club Movement as a whole was deeply significant. For the first time the unity of purposes which had inspired countless personal individualistic undertakings was recognised. Formulation gave the N.A.B.C. its place in the nation's life as a distinctive welfare organisation with a positive national objective.

'The document was hammered into agreed shape by a group composed of Colonel Campbell, L.F. Ellis, B.L.Q. Henriques and W. McG. Eagar. Its origin, however, dated back to 1917 when an Oxford and Bermondsey Club Manager, serving as a gunner, had an idle day in an observation post behind Bailleul.

'He returned to Bermondsey on demobilisation and in 1923 sent a memorandum, "Notes on the Technique of Boys' Club Management", to a few friends, but met with little encouragement.

'At length persistence won its way with reasonable men. By that time the ideas outlined in the observation post behind Bailleul had been sharpened by a post-war friendship with Colonel Ronald Campbell.

Campbell's travelling circus included as demonstrators of the fighting spirit which had to be aroused to win the war, Sergeant Wilcox, a doughty exponent of the bayonet; Ricardo Maund and other amateur boxers; the lion-hearted professional boxer, Jimmy Driscoll, and the famous padre "Woodbine Willie" who had accompanied raiding parties in order to bring back the wounded, and preached with the fervour of a prophet. This strangely composed but harmonious team inspirited and inspired officers and men in rest-camps with Campbell's doctrine of fitness of body, mind and spirit, and as the war drew to its end made an invaluable contribution to the treatment of shell-shocked soldiers. An introduction by an R.A.F. chaplain brought Campbell to see the Gordon Club, one of the Oxford and Bermondsey Boys' Clubs. It was, he said, what he had been looking for all his life. The future of Britain, saved by its men in the field, depended on the fitness, in the wide sense he had always given that word, of its boys. His doctrine of three-fold fitness fitted precisely into the working creed of the Boys Club men whom he now met for the first time. He abandoned his army career and threw his weight into the LFBC and NABC.'

The Principles and Aims ran into six editions, the last being published during 1945. After the World War II there was a tendency to dismiss the document as old fashioned. Many of the younger leaders maintained that the purposes of a club were sufficiently contained within the activities themselves, and that there was no need for directional moral and spiritual values. Indeed by the mid-sixties the Principles and Aims had largely become a document which most club leaders had heard about but which very few had ever read.

In 1974 the N.A.B.C. set up a high powered committee to review the policy of the movement. The committee reported during February 1975. The Report is wide ranging and after considering among other documents the Principles and Aims, come down firmly in favour of the old established values.

'We believe,' states the report, 'that all those things remain good and valid ... We recommend a clear unequivocal declaration by the Association that its main function remains as it has always been, to serve boys and young men by promoting their mental, physical and spiritual development through membership of Boys Clubs. To do this we must devote the full measure of our strength, our determination, our resources and our skill.'

This great restatement of the principles and aims of the movement, recognising as it does that man does not live by bread alone, but requires for all his activities overall directional standards and moral values, could lead to a revitalization of the Boys Club movement throughout the country.

5

1929 - 1946

UNIVERSITY OF EDINBURGH

In 1929 Colonel Campbell was appointed the first Director of Physical Education at the University of Edinburgh. At fifty one, he was at the peak of his powers and that year had won the British Open Sabre Championship. The origin of the appointment dated back to 1926 when a Committee, under the Chairmanship of the late Lord Constable, was set up to report on the social and physical amenities of student life at the University of Edinburgh. This Committee recommended that the University appoint a Director of Physical Education to organise and promote all aspects of physical education. The Director was not to be a games master — still less an instructor, but an Ex-Army or Naval Officer with special experience in physical education. The students themselves would continue to manage their own games through the Men's and Women's Athletic Clubs. The Director however would be *ex-officio* the adviser member of all their committees and co-operate with them in the organisation of games.

The recommendations of the Committee were adopted and the post advertised. Colonel Campbell was finally selected from a short list of three. The person most involved in persuading Colonel Campbell to apply for the post was an old Western Front friend of his, Sir Ernest Wedderburn, W.S. Sir Ernest subsequently became Deputy Keeper of the Signet and Rector's Assessor. Colonel Campbell and Sir Ernest Wedderburn had many things in common, including a keen interest in the Boy Scout movement.

It was with misgivings that the Colonel allowed his name to go forward. He was deeply attached to his Boys' Club work in London. On the other hand he was bitter at a social and political system that permitted poverty and deprivation. When Sir Ernest suggested that he should apply for the Edinburgh job Campbell realised the challenge. Here was an opportunity to influence privileged young people who in later years might be in a position to change the ills in society which were such a raw reality in the East End of London.

Colonel Mclean records in his inimitable way that it was in the slum conditions of the East End of London 'whose residents had neither the opportunity for self expression through organised games, nor the compensation of congenial work, that Campbell decided to seek in the

'University a wider audience for spreading his gospel of physical, mental and ethical correlation in human development.' It was in this missionary spirit that Campbell came to the University of Edinburgh.

Colonel Campbell was Director of Physical Education at Edinburgh University from his appointment on 1st May 1930 until his retiral in 1946. It is typical that during the whole of that period he never asked for, nor did he receive, an increase in salary.

On coming to Edinburgh the Colonel realised that a Director of Physical Education without an academic background might have difficulty in communicating with students. Consequently during his first few years he attended a full course of studies for the Degree of Master of Arts. In view of his position, however, the University exempted him from sitting the degree exams. On 16th January 1936 the University conferred upon him the Degree of Master of Arts (without examination) — a most unusual honour. The subjects studied included anatomy, physiology, psychology, psychiatry and moral philosophy. The discipline of a degree course must have thrown a great strain on a man now over fifty but he made full use of the opportunity. He analysed in depth those principles of character of which he had so much practical insight. He meticulously studied the philosophic background of such topics as fear, courage, honour, perseverance and faith, and married the theory to his practical experiences in the field. The result was a unique exposition of the attributes of human behaviour.

THE POLLOCK INSTITUTE

When Colonel Campbell came to Edinburgh there was no permanent gymnasium. The only gymnasium was one hired for three afternoons a week. There was no office, no staff except a groundsman, and no organisation for physical training beyond that afforded by various clubs playing outdoor games on inadequate grounds. Less than thirteen per cent of the undergraduates belonged to any University games or sports clubs, approximately five hundred out of four thousand.

The University had recently rejected proposals to make compulsory physical education and medical examination. This had been suggested for the purpose of providing information for gauging the standards, needs and progress of students.

Until 1934, the University hired recreational facilities mainly in the Pleasance Trust Gymnasium. In 1933 part of Minto House in Chamber Street was converted into a small gymnasium which was used daily from 9 a.m. till evening. The classes became so popular, however, that the Pleasance Gymnasium had again to be hired because of the large number of students who took advantage of the facilities.

Colonel Campbell conducted at least two classes a week himself up to the outbreak of the Second World War. At the end of each class the students were served with a peculiar body-building mixture of hot water, milk and lemon, sugar and meal, known affectionately as 'Minto House Brew' or to earlier generations of students 'Highland Brew.' One South African rugby player said of it, 'You miss it more than you appreciate it.'

The Minto House arrangements were unsatisfactory and Colonel Campbell constantly urged the University authorities to build or acquire a Gymnasium of their own.

In 1938 the Rector, Sir Donald Pollock, who was extremely interested in the work of the new department, and a great benefactor to the University, purchased premises in the Pleasance which he handed over to the University for use as a gymnasium. These buildings have an interesting history. Originally owned by a monastery, they are reputed to have been a distillery before they were occupied by Ritchie's Breweries. In turn they were taken over by Edinburgh United Breweries. The pillars which are a feature of the two large gymnasia are part of the original structure and cannot be removed. Before the premises could be fully adapted for Campbell's purposes certain alterations had to be made. A five years plan was drawn up to convert the building into two gymnasia, a fencing salle, six badminton and six squash courts, a swimming pool and a 200 yards outside running track. Work began on this project in 1938 but, with the outbreak of war in the following year, restrictions were placed on construction. Only the gymnasia and salle were completed before further work on the building ceased for the duration of the war.

The Pollock Institute opened its doors at the beginning of the Autumn term in 1940. The salle was a masterpiece and perhaps, in its day, the finest of its kind in Great Britain. During the Second World War part of the premises were used by the Ministry of Food and various Auxiliary Units. There was constant pressure on Colonel Campbell to cede the whole of the gymnasiums to the government for administrative purposes, but he successfully resisted this. His Great War experiences had taught him the morale-boosting value of recreative physical training. 'At least some recreational space is essential,' he maintained, 'in a country at war.' Twenty years after the war, Colonel Campbell's dream was finally realised. The gymnasium complex was completed with a variety of additional facilities, including the swimming pool.

THE COLONEL'S INSTRUCTORS

At Minto House, and later at the 'Pollock' Gym, Colonel Campbell gathered around him a number of hand-picked instructors, still remembered with affection by thousands of former students. The Colonel was sceptical of the professional output from the Colleges of Physical Education and none of his staff held the professional certificates which are now a normal pre-requisite for an instructor's post. They were, however, dedicated men who were to be found in the gym early in the morning and late at night — at no extra pay. Their enthusiasm pervaded the gym and they helped countless students by their encouragement and support. It did students good to come into daily contact with men who had been through the 'hards' of life. As the years rolled on, the gymnasium developed into much more than a centre of physical training — for many it became a way of life.

The Colonel's longest serving chief instructor and latterly Depute Director was Major Charles Mather. 'Charlie' Mather had served as an N.C.O. in the third Battalion of the Royal Scots. He came to Colonel Campbell's notice at the end of the Great War when he stepped forward on a troop ship and 'sorted out' the Battalion bully in thirty seconds flat. Being keen on games he was recommended for an Army physical training course at Aldershot, and quickly gained official attachment to the Corps with the rank of Sergeant. From then on he served with Colonel Campbell until the Colonel retired from the Army in 1923. Subsequently, Mather, at the Colonel's suggestion, resigned from the Army and joined him at Edinburgh University as chief instructor.

'Charlie' was good at boxing, fencing and gymnastics and had an excellent knowledge of all branches of athletics and outdoor sports. He had a flair for organisation and an uncanny sense of correct priorities. Cockney in speech, brusque in manner, and somewhat unimaginative in outlook, 'Charlie' was the man to have at your side in a tight corner. When the Colonel gave him what he thought some impossible task, 'Charlie's' eyes seemed to pop out of his head in disbelief. He would execute the task with incredible efficiency and then stand scratching his head as if finding it hard to convince himself that it had actually been done!

'Charlie' was recalled to the Army during the Second World War when he served in East Africa and the Middle East. He returned to the Gym with the rank of Major and was appointed Depute Director of Physical Training. He had a shrewd sense of judgment and helped many students in his direct no-nonsense way. Hardworking and efficient, the clock meant nothing to him in his service to others.

Tom Houston was as much a civilian in his outlook as Major Mather was an army man, and as approachable and full of fun as Charlie was brusque and prosaic. In retrospect it seems difficult to think of a more ill-assorted pair, and yet they happily worked together for many years. Tom came from one of those Leith Athletic Clubs which, during the depression, had produced champion athletes from a gym whose only facilities consisted of a cold stand pipe in an open yard. Ever since boyhood Tom had been keen on games of every kind. In due course he concentrated on gymnastics and gained international reputation as an amateur gymnast, particularly on the horizontal bar at which he excelled. He was offered an opportunity of taking part in trials for the Olympics but had to decline. His firm would not allow him the necessary time off. When Colonel Campbell came to Edinburgh, Tom attended a number of leadership courses which were organised by Colonel Campbell in the old Minto House Gymnasium. Convinced of the potential of Colonel Campbell's methods, he became one of the Colonel's most enthusiastic supporters. Later the Colonel invited him to assist as a voluntary leader. Tom accepted with alacrity and found that the experience 'enriched him beyond his imagination.' Shortly after the outbreak of the Second World War Colonel Campbell invited Tom to join his staff as acting chief instructor as Charlie Mather had been recalled to the colours. This was the start of an association which resulted in Tom being his chief instructor until the Colonel retired in 1946.

During 1945 Tom was struck down with a serious heart attack from which it seemed he might not recover. For once, the Colonel was clearly despondent. A close bond had grown up between the two men and somehow he felt personally responsible for Tom having become a professional P.T. instructor. Tom lay at death's door in the Deaconess Hospital for thirteen weeks. Late one night during the long midnight hours when Tom's spirit was at its lowest ebb, the Colonel came quietly into the ward, just as he had once appeared on the devastated battle field, and handed Tom a piece of paper on which the following words were written:

THE GOSPEL OF THE BODY
VICTORY

When you are forgotten or neglected or purposely set at naught and smile inwardly glorying in the insult — That is Victory

When your good is evil spoken; when your wishes are crossed; your taste offended; your advice disregarded; your opinions ridiculed and you take it all in loving silence — That is Victory

When you are content with any food, any raiment, any climate, any society, any solitude, any interruption — That is Victory

When you can bear with any disorder, any irregularity, any unpunctuality and annoyance — That is Victory

When you can stand face to face with waste, folly, extravagance, spiritual insensibility and endure it all as Jesus endured it — That is Victory

When you never care to refer to yourself or to record your own good works or itch after commendation; when you can truly love to be unknown — THAT IS VICTORY.

Those words illustrate vividly the fundamental attitudes of mind on which the Colonel based his life and teaching. The verses are significantly headed 'The Gospel of the Body' but they deal mainly with qualities of character. So far as the Colonel was concerned body and spirit were bound up together.

Tom made a remarkable recovery and returned to the gym although somewhat restricted in his activities. He served under Colonel Campbell's successor, Colonel Charles Usher, and died in 1975 after a short illness.

PHYSICAL TRAINING FOR WOMEN

During the Colonel's terms of office there was no full time P.T. instructor for women. Funds were short and the war hindered development of the department. The Colonel and his male instructors coped with the girls as best they could, mainly through the Womens Athletic Club. At first it was mostly the 'sporty' types who came to the gym. Charlie Mather and Tom Houston, lacking the Colonel's subtlety and accustomed to making men 'sweat' sometimes worked them too hard — with counter productive results.

Colonel Campbell realised the problem and did his best to provide the kind of women's physical training of which he approved. He employed part-time instructresses to back up Charlie and Tom. As accommodation was in short supply the women's classes were fitted into the timetable as best possible. The Colonel did not regard the situation as satisfactory and was determined to achieve a suitable scheme of recreative physical training for women.

He was a 'man's man' in a healthy way and saw the role of the sexes as different, but complementary. Young men required a robust muscular approach to physical training, while the teaching of women required emphasis on gentleness, nimbleness and grace. Effort and sweat for the men — music and rhythm for the girls.

The Colonel's approach to the training of the sexes was in tune with his attitude to all natural things. He saw nature as a divine directed rhythm with all parts in constant harmony. In this sensitive way he tried to get the training of men and women into sympathetic balance. On the other hand he was apprehensive lest men's physical education became dominated by women who were then becoming evermore influential in educational circles. As a result of the Colonel's pressure the Pollock Gym, opened in 1939, had a gymnasium for women on the second floor. The ladies gym, however, was requisitioned on the outbreak of war, and did not become available for students until the end of hostilities.

It was not until 1946 that the Colonel managed to persuade the University to increase the P.T. Staff by appointing a full time instructress.

The choice was Miss Sheila Cater.

Miss Cater was highly qualified and provided a direct link between the Womens Athletic Club and the Department of Physical Education. She introduced an extensive programme of classes for women, including fencing and Scottish Country Dancing.

She had many interests in common with Colonel Campbell, including birds and natural history. Although the last 'Campbell' appointment, Miss Cater did not in fact begin her work in the gym until after the Colonel had retired.

Shortly after the Colonel became Director, the women raised the question of a Physical Proficiency Certificate similar to that available for men. The University however postponed a decision on the matter until after the Colonel had retired. Women were at last given the opportunity to work for a certificate in 1948. The Colonel achieved more immediate success in the wider sphere of games activities within the framework of the Women's Athletic Club. The new Physical Training Department took over the supervision of the existing playing field and ground staff from the Women's Field Committee. This committee had been set up in 1921 following the grant to the Women's Athletic Club of ground at Kings Buildings. In the early 1930s a more suitable women's playing field and pavilion was acquired at Peffermill and made available for hockey and lacrosse. The acquisition of Peffermill provides the Women's Athletic Club with a focal point for their activities. The first groundsman was Mr J. B. Barclay. He and his wife lived for thirty years in the Peffermill Pavilion and were friends and confidants to generations of students. Mr Barclay died shortly after retirement but Mrs Barclay retained her interest in students for several years afterwards as supervisor of the tearoom at the Pollock Gym. The debt owed by the Womens Athletic Club to Colonel and Mrs Campbell is fully acknowledged in Colonel Usher's *Story of Edinburgh University Athletic Club* so the matter need not be pursued further here.

THE CAMPBELL SYSTEM

Colonel Campbell revitalised the attitude to physical training in the University. He recognised that physical education and academic study go hand in hand and that a University can assist in achieving high academic standards by encouraging students to develop sound physical habits. Colonel Lelean describes Campbell's basic thesis in these terms,

'As development of mental attributes is initiated by their correlative muscular movements, a suitable course of progressive physical training throughout youth and adolescence can ensure the evolution of a well-balanced mental maturity, and thus eliminate the main causes of human failure.'

Colonel Campbell's first task was to devise a physical education system which would suit the broad requirements of students and keep them interested. He approached the task with a simple, but profound, sense of purpose. 'The ultimate objective of physical education,' he said, 'should be to inculcate the qualities which will enable an individual to fulfil his obligations in life and to get the best out of it.' He played down the use of elaborate apparatus, where only a few performed and the remainder watched. It was obvious to him that most students disliked this type of exercise. On the other hand he did not base his system on bodily movement alone. He introduced mobile and inexpensive apparatus such as skipping ropes, swing bags, ship's fenders (which took the place of medicine balls and were less costly), five foot long sticks, logs varying between four and fifteen feet long, tennis balls, quoits, bicycle and motor tyres, barrels, bricks, Indian Clubs, bean bags and all manner of miscellaneous items. This approach stimulated a class and created focal points of interest and amusement.

His chief instructor, Major Mather, ran a voluntary class in advanced gymnastics for those who wished to specialise and Tom Houston gave similar instruction on the horizontal bar.

The Colonel's 'log and stick exercises' have a curious history. During the later Victorian era, German gymnasts visiting the Highland Games in Scotland were impressed by the tossing of the caber. They felt, however, that the Scots made very limited use of the caber and on their return to Germany they developed a series of exercises which made use of a heavy pole. Colonel Campbell came across these heavy pole exercises while in Germany. He realised their potential and continued their development into a series of intricate movements using poles and sticks of various sizes.

Colonel Campbell is possibly the only Briton this century to 'invent' a completely native system of physical training. Most of the systems commonly used in this country are continental in origin, i.e. Swedish drill, German gymnastics. In Colonel Campbell's case, there is no doubt that over the years he gradually brought to perfection a system of physical training all his own, based on the imaginative use of poles, sticks and other simple objects. Colonel Campbell's inventive genius in the field of physical education is such that he was the first to recognise that skipping was a useful exercise for a boxer in training. Under the 'Campbell system' it is possible to kit out a gymnasium in an imaginative way at little cost yet create the impression that the whole floor and wall area is covered with exciting apparatus. A particular advantage of a system of physical education based on simple apparatus is that many of the articles can be thrown into a large canvas bag and carried around as a portable gymnasium for use in a variety of premises.

'When money is short,' said the Colonel, 'the available funds must be invested in training teachers to use simple apparatus rather than in providing elaborate apparatus which no one can use without expert and therefore costly supervision.'

In addition, exercises from well-established systems such as 'Muller,' were combined with those which were now being evolved by Colonel Campbell, to give a greater variety of exercises. The formal method of exercising the muscles by groups was discarded and a new system devised on the threefold basis of agility, strength and dexterity.

To warm up, a 'ritual' was introduced which enabled a student to exercise every muscle in his body in a few minutes. The 'ritual' was performed at the beginning of all classes. It was based on the theory that if all the joints of the body were moved in all directions all muscles would be exercised. Thus the body would be toned up before the more strenuous activities were attempted. The 'ritual' was designed so that it could be done anywhere and at any time without supervision. The 'ritual' was based on the Colonel's personal system of exercises which he had performed every day throughout his life, even in the midst of military campaigns.

Every gym session closed with a burst of energy. The Colonel usually preferred the 'mad minute.' This involved the class charging round, over, through, up or down every conceivable piece of apparatus in the gymnasium, and being cuffed into even further activity by the Colonel. The 'minute' ended with a charge into the dressing rooms from which the next class was pouring. Next in popularity was a five minute game of 'hockey.' This was a robust knuckle damaging game of indoor hockey played with sawn off walking sticks and a tennis ball. The students who were still on their feet at the end of the game carried the casualties to the changing rooms! Basket-ball was another favourite and played with more energy than skill. Finally there was a game of volleyball played over a ten foot bar using a brick rolled in many layers of cloth and canvas. When play began the 'ball' seemed as light as a feather but at the end of the game staggering students found that it weighed a ton. Short periods of relaxation were interspersed with the sharp action. The students lay limply on the floor while the Colonel quietly directed their thoughts to the tranquility of gentle landscapes, and flowing rivers. The ability to relax and release tension is as important for total well being as physical activity.

Colonel Campbell loathed the linked free-standing exercises which were included in most P.T. tables before the Second World War and the 'ritual' included the kind of free standing exercises of which he approved. In this he was not alone. Swedish drill was championed by the Board of

Education for many years, but frequently criticised for its dullness. As practised in the early years of this century, it was a rigid and inflexible system. Teachers of physical training regarded departure from it almost as a heresy.

Self effort was the keynote of the 'Campbell' system. The instructor was the 'captain' of the team, leading his men by example, all working and thinking together. 'Thought' was also important in the system. One of Campbell's aphorisms was, 'Thought without action is a daydream, and action without thought is a form of St Vitus Dance.' The system was so devised that each participant contributed what he could in physical effort and received what he required. As a result persons of widely different ages and varying physical aptitudes could work harmoniously together for the benefit of all.

Colonel Campbell placed particular emphasis on 'foot exercises' — a legacy from his foot slogging Boer War experiences. He is said to have made his company take off their boots at every stream to massage their feet during the long marches over the South African Veldt. 'Look after your feet and your feet will look after you.' 'You grow old from your feet upwards.' 'You go out of this world feet first.' 'Give the best tempered man in the world sore feet and he becomes a fiend' — quipped the Colonel as he took his class through the ritual of the feet. There must be many oldsters today whose two feet 'Weary Willie' and 'Tired Tim' are as serviceable as ever — thanks to those exercises.

Equally important, he also had a ritual of 'eye exercises' which could be practised at odd moments and were designed to strengthen eye muscles. Colonel the Reverend Charles Scott Shaw was a former student at Edinburgh University and one of Colonel Campbell's part-time assistants — at half a crown an hour. He is now a minister in Adelaide, Cape Town. Recently he commented that Campbell was 'the most effective advocate (and practitioner) of preventive medicine that Scotland ever produced.' Colonel Campbell never failed to stress the importance of positive thinking in terms of health and not of sickness.

'The Greeks worshipped the body,' he said,
'The Romans brutalised the body — and the
 Christians reverenced the body.'

Colonel Campbell introduced into the gym a sense of fun, purpose and togetherness which had a tonic effect on those who took part in the classes. On visiting the gym the first impression was of a peculiar mixture of sweat and laughter. By trial and error the Campbell system was gradually evolved — and it was successful. Whereas in the first year of the department less than 100 students had enrolled, by 1939 the number had risen to well over 900. Notwithstanding ever increasing numbers, the gym was so organised that at almost any hour of the day students could join a class, and take a half hour of physical exercises under a skilled — and enthusiastic instructor. Today, of course, the situation has vastly changed and the average number of students using the many recreational facilities now available at the gym amount to several thousand.

The Colonel was a master of improvisation. In order to meet the need for skilled instructors, without incurring a prohibitive wages bill, he relied heavily on voluntary effort. Students attaining an essential standard of proficiency were employed to train others, in ever-widening circles, until enough expert volunteers were available to take all classes — from novices up to certificate standard.

Colonel Campbell saw the gym as the hub of all the other recreational activities and not just as one activity among others. The gym was the powerhouse that generated the robust energy on which more specialised activities depended. In an article in *The Journal of Physical Education* in July 1944, he wrote,

'The high priests of physical education should realise that the gymnasium is not a monastic institution confined to a highly specialised form of solo training. The gymnasium should be an adjunct to the classroom; it should increase the mental capacity from a physical angle.'

While encouraging outdoor sports and activities of every kind, Colonel Campbell envisaged them all as being tied in with his work in the gym where he himself presided. He maintained that field accidents could largely be avoided or mitigated, and athletic standards improved by systematic and properly directed physical training. Over the years he devised special exercises to improve performance in all sports; to assist paraplegics; and to help ordinary people in their daily work. When a student fell off a horse and injured his spine the Colonel put him on to a series of simple exercises to prevent the same thing happening again. He maintained that if foot and ankle exercises were carried out daily it was far less likely that a person would sustain a broken or twisted ankle.

The Colonel's teaching on this aspect of physical training is aptly expressed by the Edinburgh physical culturist, W. Bruce Sutherland, who wrote as early as 1917:

'Some readers may be inclined to think that games, such as football, cricket, or golf, afford a sufficient means of developing and maintaining the physique. Such athletic exercises do certainly give valuable aid in keeping the body fit, but they do not contribute much to its development, and they may even be unfavourable to its equal and symmetrical development. One expects to find strength and endurance in the leg muscles of the footballer, but chest and arm development are often weak, and where these parts are well developed it is usually due not to the practice of the game, but to the systematic physical culture which all first-class men practise as a training for the game. The playing of the game itself gives no physical culture in the scientific sense of the term any more than the work of the labourer. The mind is concentrated upon the results rather than the movements of the muscles. This is true of all games and it follows that, however much benefit to health they may bring incidentally, through the fresh air and other desirable elements which accompany their practice, they can never take the place of systematic physical culture in developing and strengthening the body.'

Colonel Campbell was well aware of the work of Bruce Sutherland. He knew Sutherland personally and was influenced by the Edinburgh man's approach to Physical Education.

At one time the Colonel's views on physical education were regarded as unorthodox if not revolutionary, but the passing years have shown that he was an original thinker in advance of his time. Many of his ideas have now been incorporated into modern systems of training. It is clear from the following excerpt from the Report of the University Grants Committee issued in 1935 that by that date his system was regarded as sound both in theory and in practice:

'In this country anything in the nature of compulsion in such a personal matter as that of physical exercises would be repugnant. On the other hand the intimate connection between the health of the mind and the health of the body is becoming increasingly recognised, and we feel that the health of the students at the Universities is a matter which cannot be ignored, and indeed in the case of certain institutions is not now ignored by the University Authorities. We incline to think that if there were in fact more adequate provision for physical training, more skilled teachers in the subject at the Universities and more scientific provision for considering individual needs and capacities in this respect — the Department of Physical Education in Edinburgh is an admirable example — a large number of students would voluntarily avail themselves of opportunities, so obviously important for their well being.'

By the mid-thirties there were many commercialised 'systems' of physical culture in vogue, some of them claiming to be unique, infallible and indispensible. Colonel Campbell never commercialised his system of physical education. He constantly improved it, and was always eager to try out new ideas, either from his own staff, or from other teachers of physical education. Indeed it was not so much a system, as a series of systems within a system involving a peculiar blend of the philosophical and the practical. That is why there is no manual of his complete work, although much is to be found in his limited publications as well as in duplicated sheets many of which still survive.

Of all the commercialised 'systems,' the Colonel's system had most in common with that of Lieutenant J. P. Muller of the Royal Danish Army who was the author of a series of best sellers including, *My System for Men, My System for Women, My System for Children,* and *My Breathing System.* Muller was born in 1866 and had studied theology before joining the Army. Later he was a civilian engineer and subsequently Inspector at the Vejlefjord Sanatorium for consumptives at Jutland. He resigned this appointment to devote himself entirely to promoting the importance of personal hygiene and to writing ethical works. He was not in favour of elaborate apparatus and in 1915 came out publicly against the then established system of Swedish drill.

By means of physical exercises and athletics he transferred himself from a delicate boy into one of the most successful all-round amateur sportsmen on the continent. In 1917, when the Colonel was serving on the Western Front, Lieutenant Muller, then aged 51, came to England. Between Putney and Hammersmith he cycled, ran, walked, paddled, sculled and swam six consecutive half miles in the record time of 29 minutes 19 2-5 secs. Colonel Campbell freely acknowledged his indebtedness to Lieutenant Muller, and personally carried out some of Muller's exercises every day, particularly his rubbing and slapping exercises. The importance of the Muller system was in its recognition of the fundamental importance of general health in all the vital, organic functions rather than in the mere development of muscular strength.

'By Physical Culture,' wrote Lieutenant Muller, 'I understand work performed with the conscious intention of perfecting the body, mind and soul and increasing one's individual health, strength, speed, staying power, agility, suppleness, courage, self-command, presence of mind and social disposition.'

In this short definition is to be found that combination of physical, mental and moral attributes which Colonel Campbell was later to take apart and then synthesise in a brilliant new concept. Muller's all-embracing system included not only natural exercises and bodily hygiene in such matters as food, clothing, and smoking, but also highlighted important factors such as 'breathing' and 'relaxation.' In addition the exercises provided for specific parts of the body such as the neck and feet.

The continental panache of Lieutenant Muller was in contrast to the metaphysical Scottish exponent of physical culture, Bruce Sutherland, whom we have already encountered. Sutherland was active in Edinburgh during the earlier years of the twentieth century. He died on 27th July, 1933, at the age of 58, four years after Colonel Campbell had taken up his appointment in Edinburgh. Bruce Sutherland had a wide circle of friends in business and professional circles and was a prominent member of the Edinburgh Rotary Club and the City Businessmen's Club. He was keenly interested in Boys' Clubs where he lectured on physical culture and gave practical demonstrations. Bruce Sutherland was an exponent of Ju Jitsu and during 1908 defeated a Japanese expert in the Waverley Market. The Colonel and Bruce Sutherland knew each other well. They often met at Boys' Clubs and in the boxing booths, common in Edinburgh and Leith during the early 1930s.

In 1917 (the same year that Lieutenant Muller carried out his record breaking performance between Putney and Hammersmith) Thomas Nelson & Sons published the Bruce Sutherland system of Physical Culture. Like Lieutenant Muller, Bruce Sutherland rejected the use of elaborate apparatus and saw the conception of physical culture in the wider context of social hygiene coupled with the mature development of the body, mind and spirit. In this he had the support of many prominent men of their day including Edinburgh's Medical Officer of Health, Dr A. Maxwell Williamson. The ghastly losses of the Great War underlined the need for developing high standards of fitness and morale, and by the time his 'System' was published, Bruce Sutherland was engaged in the physical training of countless thousands of young men all destined for the various theatres of war. This was done as a contribution to the national effort — and without fee or reward.

Bruce Sutherland envisaged physical culture as an element in complete education. He taught that while the immediate aim of physical culture is the development of the muscular system and the promotion of health, the ultimate ideal is the development of the man or woman to that perfection which is expressedin the lofty phrase: 'in the image of God.' In discussing physiological instruction which Bruce Sutherland considered an integral part of physical training he wrote:

'The whole subject (i.e. physiological instruction) should be treated on a high ideal level — self reverence, self knowledge, self control — as essential for one who would make the best of life; and as a basis for the still higher aim of making the body a temple of the Divine.'

The views of Bruce Sutherland take us another step nearer the schedule of attributes which was gradually forming in the Colonel's mind and which he crystallized into final form during the 1940s.

PHYSICAL ABILITY TESTS

As a means of encouraging students to gauge their physical ability and to help instructors to plan suitable exercises, a series of twelve experimental tests were introduced. After much research these were reduced to eight, based on agility, strength and dexterity. They were the standing high and long jumps, full press up, heaving fender forward and downward between the legs, throwing a tennis ball at a target placed ten foot high on the wall, throwing quoits on to a hub and a sprint. There were four grades: (a) pass (b) average (c) first class and (d) special. The standards were plainly marked in the gym so that students without supervision could see for themselves the progressive results of their efforts. Record cards were kept for each student.

Over the years a student could improve his physique by working systematically at the tests, which have now been superseded by a somewhat different system. Colonel Campbell continually experimented with his tests and for a time carried out a large number of measurements with a view to achieving 'a co-efficient of physical efficiency' which would be used as a simple yardstick to gauge the 'vital capacity' of every individual. This was to be achieved by reducing to a decimal figure information based on a student's chest expansion in relation to his weight in pounds, plus his height in inches. In this, he may have been influenced by a study entitled *The Assessment of Physical Fitness* by Georges Dreyer and George Fulford Hanson, published by Cassell and Company in 1920. This study involved the assessment of physical fitness by the correlation of vital capacity with certain measurements of the body. Colonel Campbell eventually discarded his experiments, after prolonged research had shown that his results were statistically inconclusive.

The Colonel placed great emphasis on the physical ability tests, particularly on the recording of the results so that each student had his own continuing progress report. Writing in 1938 he said:

'Measurement is fundamental to every science; this applies to Physical Education, the science of bodily movement. By means of measurement the value and results of Physical Education can be assessed, correlated with mental education and directed accordingly. Without measurement to guide it and help it on its course, Physical Education would lose its direction and dissipate much of its force.'

THE CERTIFICATE OF PHYSICAL PROFICIENCY

One of Campbell's outstanding achievements at the University was the introduction of the Certificate of Physical Proficiency. Research had been carried out for a number of years beforehand. The first course was inaugurated in 1938 with the approval of the University Court. At that time Edinburgh was the only University in the world which provided a Certificate of Physical Proficiency free to any matriculated student who was prepared to undertake the work of the course and achieve a certain standard.

To qualify for the examination students had to attend the gym thirty times between October and March (about three times a fortnight), attain 60% in the basic tests and be able to swim one length of the swimming bath. Training of a specialised nature was given in the Summer Term to those who had qualified and an examination conducted by two outside examiners was held on a suitable day during the first week in June.

The first examination was held in June 1939 and six students took part. Only two passed and on Graduation Day they became the first to hold the Certificate. One of them was Dr George Malloch, now a Medical Practitioner in the south side of Edinburgh. To mark the occasion the Colonel asked the successful candidates for photographs of themselves for exhibition in the Pollock Gym. George Malloch posed for the photograph in his gym singlet and shorts which he thought the proper gear for the holder of a Certificate of Physical Proficiency. It is a curious aspect of Colonel Campbell's character that for months afterwards he tried to persuade Dr Malloch to have his photograph re-taken in academic dress. Unorthodox as he was in many ways, the Colonel just could not accept the idea of one of his first graduates appearing in an official photograph 'improperly dressed.'

The Certificate was a striking innovation in University circles. Edinburgh became the only Scottish university where a student could obtain not only an academic degree, but a certificate course intended to produce all round fitness with some ability to train others to become and keep fit. Since 1960 the Certificate of Physical Proficiency has been replaced by a two year extra curricular course leading to the unique University of Edinburgh Award in Physical Education. This requires not only theoretical consideration of the role of physical education and sport in modern society but also practical experience of four main outdoor and indoor skills. The aim of the course is to equip students to act as amateur but informed physical leaders in any community to which they may belong after leaving the University.

THE SPORTS SECTIONS

As was to be expected from a man of Colonel Campbell's versatile mind new forms of physical activity were introduced into the curriculum.

A fencing section was formed in 1930 and affiliated to the Edinburgh University Athletic Club. The Colonel's life-long interest in fencing is referred to more fully in a later chapter. Judo was introduced in 1938. W. Holman, an experienced Judo expert who had been a member of the Judo Club at Oxford, came to Edinburgh to study agriculture, and Colonel Campbell persuaded him to pioneer the sport in Edinburgh. In spite of the enthusiasm and keenness of a few students Judo did not become popular until the end of the Second World War, when interest in the sport revived. Kasumi, the renowned Japanese Judo expert, then resident in Britain, supervised one of the first grading contests in

Scotland. It was held in the Pollock Gym during the early 1940s.

At that time Judo involved attitudes which appealed to the Colonel's concepts of sportsmanship. There was no Judo champion. All contests whether inter-club or individual, were on a friendly basis. The teacher or 'master' of a class was never beaten by his pupil — no matter how far the pupil finally outclassed the master.

It was considered unladylike for women to participate in the sport except to learn certain tricks of self defence. Knowledge of the disabling or killing blows was forbidden until Black Belt standard had been achieved. Finally, the sport involved rules of personal conduct and cleanliness which are still recognised by exponents of the art.

It was a long time before the University Judo Club had proper equipment. Initially, four gym mats were locked together and secured by a tarpaulin. This worked well enough until the mats gradually drifted apart under the tarpaulin and the unfortunate participants received unexpected cracks as they landed on the hard floor. It was all part of the fun.

Basketball was also sponsored by Colonel Campbell. To begin with it was often played in a rough and ready form during P.T. periods. It was another of the Colonel's Great War ideas picked up from the Canadians and Americans. Orthodox basketball was introduced by American students at the then Royal College of Surgeons. They played it as early as 1930/3. Although not matriculated at Edinburgh University they were encouraged and given facilities in the gym by Colonel Campbell. Few students other than Americans 'cottoned on' to this sport until after the Second World War. Basketball then began to be played throughout Britain. After Colonel Campbell retired in 1946 a section was formed and affiliated to the Athletic Club with successful results.

Colonel Campbell was a good archer. He claimed that archery provided relaxation in the midst of a busy life. On occasional summer afternoons, accompanied by his students, he practiced at Canal Field, Peffermill, or in George Square Gardens. A picnic lunch was a feature of those glorious afternoon excursions, where the day passed in alternative bouts of shooting and discussion. During the winter makeshift indoor butts were set up in the basement of the Minto House Gym but they were not much used. He was invited to join the Royal Company of Archers but declined owing to the high cost.

The Colonel supported every physical activity organised by the students. He joined the Scottish Country Dance class in which he performed well and with great enthusiasm.

He allowed the S.R.C. to use the gym for dances. The students could have it as late as they wanted (within reason) subject to one condition, which was absolute. The gym had to be in immaculate working order by

8.30 am the following morning. This condition never caused difficulty and for about an hour and a half after every dance members of the S.R.C. worked off their surplus energy in moving equipment, cleaning floors and ensuring that the gym was in apple pie order before they left in the early hours of the morning.

The Colonel took a keen interest in the annual race up Arthur's Seat. The race to the top of the Lion's Head originated in 1924. It commenced at the Union in Teviot Place and the course lay through St Leonards to the Park gate in St Leonard's Bank. From there it was straight up to the top and down again via the Gutted Haddie and then back through the streets to the Union. Times ranged between 19 and 22 minutes. The Colonel often acted as starter and was almost inevitably accompanied by Colonel Lelean. Colonel Lelean surpassed Colonel Campbell in enthusiasm for this event — even trundling after the competitors on an old bicycle. There was something about the race that fascinated the Colonel. Perhaps it was sheer effort of will needed to drive the competitor to the top of the hill and then force his weary steps back to the Union. Certainly the event separated the men from the boys. 'If I were asked to get together a team to undertake some impossible task,' the Colonel once confided, 'I would take the last twelve Arthur Seat Winners — they would be unbeatable.'

As a former Army boxing champion, Colonel Campbell went out of his way to encourage boxing in the University. Later he became sensitive to the possibility of brain damage and took more interest in judo. In the early 30s the boxing sections employed two colourful instructors from Charlie Cotter's wellknown boxing club in Leith Street. Paddy Fee was a boxing philosopher who spoke, ate and drank boxing. He was a silver medalist in the 1908 Olympic Games, a Scottish light-weight champion and a contemporary of the redoubtable Tancy Lee. There were giants in the ring in those days. He influenced generations of youngsters and he lived on to the ripe old age of 92. He was an ideal teacher who knew every trick of the trade and had the knack of doing as little as possible to achieve amazing results. He slouched into the gym, hands in pockets, shoulders hunched, and in many ways was the very antithesis of the Colonel. He spoke little, but what he said was full of meaning. Where Paddy Fee left off, his pal Bill Samuels took over.

Bill was a motivated pugilist who knocked his brains out pushing the students to higher standards of performance. Paddy Fee and Bill Samuels haunted the gym for many years and added colour to the boxing section of the Athletic Club.

It was Bill Samuels who gave Colonel Campbell the most embarrassing moment of his life. Bill had been unwell for some time and the Colonel went to see how he was keeping. Finding him on the point of recovery he he suggested that they go for a walk. Bill readily agreed, and the pair left Bill's house in the Pleasance and walked along Princes Street. It was a sunny day, but bitterly cold. The Colonel suggested to Bill that he might like to go to the pictures. Bill demurred as he had never visited a cinema in his life. 'There must always be a first time,' said the Colonel and took Bill into the old Palace Cinema in Princes Street. In the 30s the Palace was a rather genteel cinema, visited in the afternoon by ladies of leisure and the occasional businessman. It mainly showed news films and cartoons. Entering the darkened auditorium from sunny Princes Street poor Bill found himself in a strange environment. Blundering down the aisle behind the usherette his raucous voice disturbed the patrons. 'What the hell's that light shining in my eyes?' The Colonel quickly grabbed him by the arms and manoeuvred him to a convenient seat. Sensing the mutterings around him the Colonel glanced at Bill. Bill was a tall man and, not appreciating that the seats tipped up, was perched on the top edge blocking the view of the patrons behind. The Colonel manoeuvred him forward and was in the process of folding down the seat when Bill suddenly slithered forward and crashed under the seat in front. To complete the Colonel's misery there flashed on to the screen the opening sequences of Walt Disney's 'Pluto'. As Bill noisily struggled into a sitting position he said loudly, 'That's a hell o' a funny dug, Colonel.'

PROPHET IN PLIMSOLES

Physical skills in isolation were relatively unimportant to Colonel Campbell. Behind every physical movement of the body he saw the 'psychic equivalent' and his philosophy involved the mature growth not only of the body but also of the mind and spirit. During his work in London with the Boys' Club movement, Colonel Campbell had gradually crystallized much of his basic thinking into written form. The following extract from a pamphlet on *Fitness* written in 1928 for the London Division of the Church Lads' Brigade illustrates his practical insight into human activity, as well as a vivid literary style.

'Every physical movement produces a definite impression on the mind. A balance exercise is the physical expression of self-control: the physical to the moral is only a change of gear. If the arm is slowly bent with a concentrated effort, the movement is suggestive of endurance and concentration of purpose. A vigorous outward or striking action of the limbs stimulates energy and creates a sense of decision; the raising of a limb slowly or quickly is suggestive of a moral calmness; the reaching upwards with the arms has an elevating effect on the mind. Slow rhythmic movements are soothing to the mind and predispose the mind to patience and tolerance, while a quick rotating of the limbs exhilarates and stimulates a feeling of cheerfulness. In fact every physical expression has a psychic equivalent; the very pose and shape of our body was created and is an expression of thought.

Do not slide into the habit of allowing thoughts to evaporate into idle day-dreams or merely to arouse the emotions. An emotion is a mobilization of nervous force for action; it is an explosion of power and should not be used as a round of blank ammunition at the burial service of some good intention. The emotional habit soon degenerates into a harmful one of self-indulgence and sentimentality; it is a leakage of nervous force and undermines the character.'

The broad background of national character and fitness against which Campbell saw his work in the gym is clearly envisaged in passages which occur earlier in the same pamphlet.

'When a people begins to live on credit, on its past traditions, and does not pay cash down in energy, inspiration and ideals, it ceases to pay its debt to the world. It is only a matter of time before it becomes a moral bankrupt and is discredited before the other nations. This is no far-fetched theory open to doubt or argument; it is one of the most striking and relentless lessons of history.

The red light of national decadence is material prosperity. The decline of a nation comes with the worship of wealth and the lowering of life's ideals, with ostentatious luxury and the insidious contamination of slums. No cunning use of rouge and powder will for long hide or stay the ravages of an internal disease.

The first duty of every patriot is as plain and straightforward as is the first lesson learnt in the field of sport, which is to get fit and keep fit in order to play the game for the side. But fitness must not be confined to the playing fields or be regarded as the fetish of a health crank, it is the bed-rock of national existence, it is the one guarantee of good faith which nature demands of us.

What is meant by fitness? It is something simple and concrete, a healthy mind in a healthy body — a moral force supported by physical power.'

Colonel Campbell's reference to the duties of a patriot in the article reflect his Great War morale-boosting techniques. After this Colonel Campbell does not refer to patriotism in quite the same way — even during the second World War. By the late twenties he was looking towards international understanding and to co-operation between competing elements in society on a world-wide scale.

Colonel Campbell contended that character could be created 'drop by drop' as a bucket is gradually filled with water. For that reason he hated trivial conversation in the gym or anywhere else. He rarely discussed his students' academic progress. He took it for granted that they would pass their exams and his whole system was designed to assist them to that end. His conversation was positive and often directed to finding out what his students were doing for the community. There was no dodging Campbell. Everyone was expected to be doing something worthwhile to help others. This spirit pervaded the gym. Colonel Campbell's conception of community work meant regular involvement on a committed basis. He considered that much of what passed as community work was little more than an exercise in self-indulgence.

Colonel Campbell's views were not haphazard but were systematically worked out and reduced to a schedule of attributes in diagramatic form. The schedule is reproduced towards the end of the book.

The schedule was compiled over the years and put into final shape during July 1942. The original charts were prepared with the help of Colonel's chief instructor, Tom Houston. The 'unveiling' of the schedule during the darkest period of the war was not accidental. Campbell saw clearly that the ultimate threat to the nation was not Hitler's Germany, but the insidious undermining of national character.

The schedule is a remarkable blend of philosophical insight and practical experience. It is a culmination of forty years work and a unique contribution to the study of human behaviour.

'Body, mind and spirit,' contended the Colonel, 'function together, and for true fulfilment they require systematic development as a totality. The starting point is in physical movement, proceeding by gradations to nobility of character. To begin with we are essentially physical, then the intellect develops, gradually maturing during the fullness of life into the enduring qualities of personal character. We depart life in the reverse manner. As old age approaches the first faculties to deteriorate are the physical — then the intellect, and last, showing in our faces as we reach the end of the road, are those qualities of character which are immortal.'

In the *Psychological Aspect of Physical Education*, published in 1939 he wrote —

'There can be a glory in the sunset of life, lit up by bright rays of mental and moral beauty.'

That is the background against which Campbell's schedule of attributes must be considered. Each group of attributes is modified or controlled by those immediately above and below. The concepts can easily be understood without the aid of elaborate exposition. The lower group in the table comprise fundamental *physical* attributes such as 'health,' 'versatility' and 'vitality' moving upwards to such qualities of the intellect as 'education,' intelligence' and 'judgment.' The highest group of attributes are those of the *spirit* — 'faith,' 'truth,' and ultimately 'tolerance' and 'nobility' of character.

In devising his schedule the Colonel envisaged a systematic progression throughout life from the purely physical to a flowering in maturity of high qualities of personal character. Such a development, based on the three-fold linkage of body, mind and spirit, did not happen by chance, but was the product of enlightened teaching by all the agencies of society including the home, church and school.

Colonel Campbell explained his schedule with quiet intensity. Beginning with those qualities mainly associated with physical activity he then went on to analyse the attributes of the mind. Finally he expounded on the great qualities of the 'spirit.' The first quality of the spirit was 'faith.' There was no ecclesiastical vagueness about Campbell. He systematically took the attributes of faith apart. The words themselves seemed to come alive as he spoke, 'hope,' 'ambition,' 'zest,' 'reverence,' 'self-fulfillment' and 'inspiration.' After discussing each of those concepts in turn he paused. 'Faith by itself,' he would then continue, 'is not enough. Faith is purposeless unless it is based on truth.' Off he would go again expounding on the separate attributes of 'truth.' After discussing the importance of 'truth' he would point out that if 'truth' was to be effective it required the support of 'energy.' It was not enough to know 'the truth.' 'There were,' he commented 'many who know the truth, or believe in the truth, but will not bestir themselves to do anything about it. For true fulfillment more than truth is needed — Energy.' But energy serves little purpose unless it is controlled by self restraint.' And so he would continue right up to the top of the chart. Here were enshrined the twin virtues of tolerance and nobility of character. 'Sympathy,' 'thoughtfulness,' 'understanding,' 'unselfishness,' and 'generosity.' Those aspects of the spirit were the ultimate achievement of mankind. The goal to which we struggle through youth, manhood and declining years.

The Colonel would enthrall an audience with his ideas. In rapt silence his confidential tones reached and inspired all who heard him.

The schedule is a constant source of inspiration for those concerned with the art of leadership and the formation of character.

Colonel Campbell's views on the therapeutic benefit of communal recreative physical training are equally striking. In the course of an article on 'Community Physical Training' which appeared in *The Journal of Physical Education* for July 1944, he wrote:

'Physical training should develop a spirit of co-operation, teamwork and leadership. These qualities have a social value and are the foundations of community life and citizenship.'

Earlier in the same article he states —

'A plan of training to include all people, men and women, boys and girls, cripples and athletes, should range from simple basic movement to difficult and complex activities. The exercises should be natural actions which have a practical value, and can be associated with life and have a bearing on its different aspects and occupations, on our works, our recreations and our household jobs. It must be simple in technique, accommodation, equipment and leadership.

Colonel Campbell placed particular emphasis on qualities of leadership.

'Every man,' he taught, 'has within him the capabilities of leadership and is a natural leader. He was created by the Almighty to look after a family, and the family is a difficult team to lead. Small children look up to older children, and so it is throughout life. Each person is regarded as an example by someone else and in that sense is a leader. The purpose of physical training is to develop to the full the individual's latent powers of leadership and that is best achieved by example. There are, of course, leaders — and leaders of leaders — and leaders of leaders of leaders.' Colonel Campbell reckoned that everyone has within him the potentialities of leadership and his entire system of physical training is directed to developing to the full an individual's innate qualities.

'Discipline' is an essential element in leadership. The 'discipline' envisaged by Colonel Campbell is not imposed from above. It is an inner quality of the mind and spirit — ' a free gift from a free person.'

When discussing 'leadership' the Colonel did not mince words. No matter how humble the level of leadership, an individual was expected to develop his or her latent ability in full. The man with one talent had to make no less effort to exercise that talent than the man with ten. Self-discipline is the key to leadership and a nation depends on the will-power of its citizens.

In a forceful article entitled 'The Compelling Force' published during his army inspectorate in *The Journal of the Army School of Physical Training*, Colonel Campbell writes:

'Will, decision, and the power of concentration, are among the essential characteristics of leadership. Without them a man is mentally flabby, undecided, incapable of assimilating and imparting knowledge, and utterly useless as an instructor or leader, however subordinate.'

This is strong stuff which the Colonel elaborates further on in the same article.

'The mind is influenced in some degree by everything it perceives. A squad, in time, will reflect the character of its instructor, in much the same way as the physical movements of a man reflect the character of his brain. If the instructor is slow of thought, undecided, lacking in driving power, he will convert a good squad into a bad one. If he is quick, alert, virile, full of tact and of compelling energy, he may raise a poor squad almost to his own level. 'An army of stags led by a lion is better than an army of lions led by a stag.' It is the power and personality of the instructor which build the character of his squad, which develop their willpower, which are projected from him into them and which compel them to concentrate all their mental energy upon their work.'

The Colonel believed in participation at all levels of community activity but only in such a disciplined manner as enables the community to benefit from its massive reservoir of latent leadership and inspired excellence. Participation involves responsibility, and responsibility recognises a hierarchy of enlightened leadership. 'Leadership,' he said, 'is the heartbeat of any successful community effort. It is the pulse of social unity.' There was a definition of a 'sportsman' which Colonel Campbell loved to recite and a copy of this definition occupied a prominent place in the gym. The definition was drawn up at a meeting representative of all ranks, lasting five hours, at the Army School of Physical Training, Aldershot, on the occasion of an Inter-Theatre of War Championships held in the United Kingdom in 1919, with representatives from the Home Forces; British Expeditionary Forces France, Egypt and Mesopotamia, taking part. It ran as follows:

A sportsman plays the game for the game's sake,

A sportsman plays for his team and not for himself,

A sportsman is a good winner and a good loser, modest in victory and generous in defeat.

A sportsman accepts all decisions in a proper spirit

A sportsman is chivalrous towards a defeated opponent; is unselfish and always ready to help others to become proficient.

As a spectator the sportsman applauds good play on both sides.

A sportsman never interferes with referee or judge no matter what the decision.

After repeating the definition Colonel Campbell would look at the listener for a moment and then say quietly: 'Are those not the qualities of the Master himself? Go away and think about it.'

Whether or not they represent the qualities of the Master they are a remarkable tribute to the idealism of a large body of men drawn from all walks of life, many of whom had seen the more vicious side of man's nature during the previous few years.

In 1939 Colonel Campbell was invited to address the Annual Meeting of the British Association. He chose as his theme: 'The Psychological Aspect of Physical Education' and worked hard at the text for many months. The anticipated lecture was something of an ordeal for him and he rehearsed variations of the address to members of the family — a most unusual action. The meeting which had been arranged for 5th September was cancelled as a result of the outbreak of the second World War and the address was never delivered although it was subsequently published in

The Edinburgh Medical Journal. Writing in the full strength of his intellectual maturity Colonel Campbell hammers home his three-fold doctrine for the benefit of posterity.

'Mind, body and spirit are as interdependent as flame, fuel and heat in a fire; one helps to create the other. So, if Physical Education develops aright, bodily, mental and moral qualities are simultaneously stimulated.'

Later in the address he illustrates his theme from a lifetime of practical experience in the gym.

'The close correlation between the mind and movement can be observed in a class under instruction in Physical Training. By watching the actions of the individuals in it, a shrewd insight into their state of mind, temperament and character can be obtained. The quick-witted can be distinguished from the dull, the adroit from the clumsy and awkward; the individual who has dash and daring shows up conspicuously in comparison to the nervous and timid; those with grit and endurance, often clumsy and awkward, can be distinguished from those who are lacking these stable qualities, often the adroit and agile; the keen and energetic show up above the idle and slack and so on. It is the thought, and spirit behind the action which gives it its force and expression.'

The Colonel never ceased to explore the underlying relationships between body, mind, and spirit. Even after retiral, the prophet in plimsoles continued to test his theories whenever he had the opportunity — in the gym, in the youth club, or in the home.

THE ASSAULT AT ARMS

To stimulate interest and to advertise the Department of Physical Education, Colonel Campbell staged a yearly 'Assault at Arms.' This was a display of physical training presented in the McEwan Hall with all Campbell's genius for the informal and dramatic. Items included displays of physical training (university system), acrobatics, German gymnastics, fencing, boxing, judo, quarter-staff, single sticks, national and folk dancing, wrestling, basketball, ski-ing and displays of life-saving by the University Rover Scouts. The shows were open to the public and a small charge made for the benefit of charity.

Colonel Campbell had a gift of improvisation and a sense of the dramatic as illustrated by the following story of Major Mather. Campbell told his staff that part of a programme would comprise of a tent pitching contest between teams of students. His staff thought that this was impossible in the McEwan Hall but Colonel Campbell chuckled and said nothing. Sure enough when the assault took place the tents were there with bricks attached to the ends of guy lines. Two teams of students then rushed into the arena and competed in erecting the two tents. The crowd roared with laughter as the drunken contraptions began to take shape on the floor of the McEwan Hall. At a whistle from the Colonel the two teams sprinted into the tents, the lights went out and a green and red light went on in each tent. In the hushed silence a piper in the darkness marched round the two dimly lit tents playing a lament. This simple display was one of the dramatic highlights of the whole show. The 'Assaults' ceased at the outbreak of war in 1939 and were revived for a short time in 1950. They have now been discontinued.

'WHO'S WHO'

Another of Colonel Campbell's University innovations was *The Varsity Athletic News* [*'VAN'*] which was distributed free to publicise student recreational facilities. After the outbreak of war VAN was incorporated into *The Student*. In 1937, Colonel Campbell launched a student's *Who's Who*. The first issue, published by Oliver & Boyd, was described as a pioneer venture and cost sixpence. It contained a section on University societies and their office bearers, as well as an alphabetical list of all the students at the University. The *Who's Who* recorded the address and country of each student and other useful information about the student's activities at the University. The Foreword to the first edition stated that the register was offered to the University somewhat tentatively in the hope that it would prove informative, interesting and even entertaining. It would enable students to see from how many places their contemporaries were drawn and would provide a record of their University days to look back on after they had graduated.

Attention was drawn to the fact that the publication was a pioneer effort and that it was hoped to establish the *Who's Who* as an annual institution to be published every January. The second edition of *Who's Who* appeared in January 1938 but publication ceased on the outbreak of war, and was never revived.

THE STUDENT HEALTH SERVICE

The Student Health Service was founded in 1929. It was another recommendation of the Constable Report. The formation of the Health Service was largely due to the dynamic effort of the late J.J.M. Shaw, F.R.C.S. It was inaugurated along with Colonel Campbell's new Department of Physical Education. The medical department shared limited accommodation provided in the Physical Education Department in Minto House. The Colonel, or a member of his staff, was always present to carry out the physical measurements of the students who were having routine medical examination. In this way Colonel Campbell developed close personal contact with all men students who passed through the medical department. At that time the women students were examined by Dr Dorothea Walpole in the Students Union. Dr J. K. Slater was the first doctor to the medical service and was joined by the late Dr R E Verney in 1932.

Campbell kept students continually informed of the Health Service and of the facilities available in the gym. He was also the originator of the annual reception for freshers at which they are welcomed by the Principal.

One of the purposes of the freshers' reception was to enable newcomers to the University to meet the secretaries of the various clubs and enrol as members. Campbell was one of the principal speakers. His speech was short and to the point.

'Our training is voluntary, full of life, and carried out in the spirit of our games. It is recreative because it is a suitable and natural reaction to class studies; it puts zest into tired brains after a spell of mental effort. The student wants a degree. Our training helps him to achieve that purpose.'

Apart from his great interest in the Student Health Service, Colonel Campbell was a regular visitor to the students' ward in the Royal Infirmary. His visits were much looked forward to and he never failed to boost the morale of the patients. Colonel Lelean records that Campbell's 'experience in London hyper-sensitised rather than inured him to human distress.' Consequently no word ever reached him of any student being ill, in want, or in trouble, without his taking prompt action in rescue or relief. He had a standing arrangement with the Royal Infirmary which enabled him to visit any student within hours of his being admitted.

Campbell's welfare work for students was very much appreciated by his contemporaries, and fathers often sent 'mixed up kids' to be straightened out. His usual cure was to get them down to the gym or back to nature in some of his outdoor activities. He had tremendous faith in the healing power of 'the wilderness.'

THE WILDERNESS CLUB

To claim that Colonel Campbell was the father of the modern trend to outdoor education would be an exaggeration, but there is little doubt that in this field, as in many others, he was well ahead of his time.

In the spring of 1937 Colonel Campbell gathered round him a group of students who were interested in all kinds of country recreations. His aim was to gradually built a series of clubs, loosely linked to the University

Athletic Club and ranging from ski-ing and mountaineering on the one hand to ornithology and botany on the other. In the period up to the outbreak of war, the club consisted mainly of Arts Faculty students who were interested in natural history but not seriously enough to join one of the societies at Kings Buildings which housed most of the Science departments.

Informal meetings were held in Minto House over a cup of coffee on Saturday evenings when outings and projects were discussed and notes compared. The main activities, however, were in 'the wilderness' and here Colonel Campbell's contacts with landowners in the Lothians and Fife gave openings the club would not otherwise have had. Expeditions included camping weekends at Lindores Loch and Edgelaw, a trip to the Isle of May and a rowing expedition aimed at Inchmickery in the Firth of Forth but which nearly ended in disaster. Those who accompanied Campbell on these expeditions into the lonely depths of the Scottish countryside were fascinated with his immense knowledge of wild life, especially of birds.

Like so many projects sponsored by Campbell those excursions served the dual object of encouraging physical fitness and a sense of adventure in students, many of whom were not interested in organised athletics, and also of widening their knowledge of the world about them.

'The phase of imaginative activity which manifests itself in boyhood cannot find satisfaction in realities, but yearns for heroic expression — an urge which should be made use of in Physical Education, and given every opportunity of a practical outlet in such outdoor activities as are natural to this age. The training which is carried out in the gymnasium should be associated with and help to fulfil the wider interests outside.'
[*The Psychological Aspects of Physical Education*]

It is interesting to compare these observations with the views of the Director of Education in Edinburgh on the objectives of outdoor education as contained in a Comprehensive Memorandum submitted to Edinburgh Education Committee during March 1972.

'There are two main objectives (to outdoor education) firstly to widen horizons and stimulate attitudes to study society and our environment within an increasingly broad school curriculum, and secondly to prepare for lasting and worthwhile interests and values in adulthood.'

Another aspect of Colonel Campbell's encouragement of physical activity including outdoor recreation particularly among young people was his practical recognition that:

'It is during adolescence ... when the body is making its fastest sprint, that the mind also is rocked by new and disturbing emotions, and therefore requires to be helped and balanced and not allowed to be driven by the emotions into dangerous channels.'

Colonel Campbell envisaged the gym as a gateway to the vast field of outdoor recreative activity and the consequential benefits which accrue as a result of a controlled development of the body from infancy into adolescence. The Colonel's teaching on the problems of the growing adolescent goes to the root of the matter and have scarcely been bettered.

'It is important that in the period of the greatest physical development as well as the awakening of the sexual impulses, there should be an appropriate welding of the two forces. The creation of a healthy physical appetite and zest for physical effort will predispose the mind towards manly qualities and stability of character.'

Colonel Campbell had the gift of drawing the best out of people and infecting them with his enthusiasm. The most diffident student would find himself organising a 'wilderness' expedition of major proportions, and doing it successfully. Through the Wilderness Club he quietly developed in many of his students quite unsuspected powers of leadership, observation, and endurance, which in later years have stood them in good stead.

THE MASTERY OF ONE'S SELF

Colonel Campbell was a man of quiet Christian faith. Like the Master, he was usually in Church on Sundays. He was early in his pew where he sat meditating as the congregation gathered. When resident in Edinburgh, he attended Greyfriars where he was a friend of the minister, the Reverend Dr D.W.P. Strang, whom he held in the highest regard. The deeply philosophical side of his nature was tempered with a tremendous sense of fun which often overcame the opposition of people who were hostile to his ideas. Practical jokes were the salt of his life and were perpetrated on friends, complete strangers and his own family.

During an Assault-at-Arms at Salen one of his young sons gave a boxing exhibition. In the middle of the demonstration a drunk tinker blundered into the tent. 'Come over here,' rapped the Colonel, 'and this young boy will soon sort you out.' The tinker lurched to the platform and grappled with the child while the terrified spectators yelled for the police. After a short scuffle the boy knocked the false nose off the drunk unmasking one of the Colonel's friends, dressed up for the part.

He even pulled the leg of an American fencing team which visited Britain in 1930. In 1921 Campbell had captained a British fencing team which had toured the United States. In 1930 the American team returned the visit and Campbell had the distinction of being made Honorary Captain of the American team. He arranged for the visitors to be accommodated at the R.A.C. Club in London and for their reception by

King George V at Buckingham Palace. He instructed the visiting team to wear top hats for the Palace visit and ordered a supply of toppers from Moss Brothers for them to select. After parading the team along Pall Mall and Victoria Street in top hats, he said cheerfully; 'All right, lads — you can put the hats away — it's just a bit of fun.'

In 1941 an incident occurred that highlighted Colonel Campbell's complex personality. It was the custom for Tom Houston to report to the Colonel every morning when the day's work in the gym was discussed. 'Excuse me, sir,' said Tom, 'but are you quite yourself this morning?' Tom had noticed that instead of his normal good colour the Colonel was ashen grey. The Colonel ignored the interruption and continued to discuss the day's work.

At the end of the interview, instead of dismissing Tom in his customary manner, the Colonel looked at him keenly and remarked: 'So you think I am not looking so well?' 'No, sir,' said Tom, 'you are definitely under the weather.'

The Colonel sat silent for a moment, while tears rolled down his cheeks. 'Tom,' he said, 'this is a terrible day for me. My son Bruce is a conscientious objector and I am going to London tonight to speak for him before a Tribunal.'

The misery of the Colonel was so complete that nothing more was said between the two men and Tom slipped quietly away. The Colonel went to London that night and stayed in his London Club. The next morning he appeared before the Tribunal and spoke for his son. There he stood — Boer War veteran, Western Front legend, and former Inspector of the Army School of Physical Training, pleading for his son before a Conscientious Objectors' Tribunal. What it cost him no one will ever know.

'My son's work as a physical training instructor,' he said, 'has given him such a reverence for the whole man that he cannot now bring himself to take human life.'

The Colonel's testimony resulted in his son being granted conditional exemption from the Military Register. During the whole of this episode the Colonel never breathed to his son a word of criticism or reproach. In some ways it was his finest hour.

On returning to Edinburgh, he said nothing. Many months later, however, when talking with Tom in the gymnasium he quietly changed the subject and said, 'Tom — do you remember my telling you that my son was a conscientious objector and that I had to go to London to plead his cause?' 'Yes,' replied Tom, 'but you never told me what happened.' 'No,' said the Colonel, 'but I will tell you this. Ever since I went to London I have been thinking about my son's stand in regard to military service, and do you know something Tom, I'm not sure but that the boy isn't right!'

Throughout his life the Colonel must have been constantly at war with himself. On the one hand he was a warrior who feared neither death nor the devil. On the other, he was an idealist who devoted much of his life to the 'underdog' and encouraging people to find self-fulfilment in their own way.

Tom Houston remembered another incident which emphasises the Colonel's quiet modesty as well as his conern for others. Early one winter morning Tom was cycling down to the Pollock Gym. Snow was falling and had already carpetted the ground. Ahead of him in Hill Street he saw the Colonel walking through the snow carrying a sack across his shoulders. Scurrying along at his side was an old rag woman. Tom dismounted and followed the Colonel at a safe distance.

The Colonel and the rag woman continued down the Pleasance and into the Cowgate where they entered a scrap merchant's yard. The Colonel heaved the sack on to the scales, touched his cap to the rag woman and quietly slipped her a coin. He then walked off through the snow and back to the gym to greet the first of the students arriving for the day.

Colonel Campbell had the same caring relationship with students as with the ex-servicemen in the streets of London. There was one aspiring athlete, Dick Rawlinson, who struggled for many years to achieve an athletic blue. He plodded round the Meadows during the cold winter evenings; trotted up Arthur's Seat at 7.30 a.m. and turned out religiously with the 'Hare and Hounds' on Wednesday and Saturday afternoons. His standard gradually improved and finally he was awarded a full blue.

Like many others of his generation this particular student was impoverished and depended entirely on his parents for support. The thought of purchasing a blazer simply did not occur to him. He considered the possibility of a tie, but even the price of a tie was out of the question. Entering the gym some days after the award he encountered Colonel Campbell. The Colonel looked at him with his steely blue eyes, and then held out a gnarled hand. 'Congratulations, Dick,' he said, 'sheer guts and hard effort.' As Dick's heart swelled with pride he looked down, and found in his own hand the gleaming blue and white of the coveted tie.

During the second World War the Colonel organised a course for training youth leaders at Carstairs. One evening while travelling there by train with Tom Houston, the two men were joined in the carriage by a young lady of means, with whose family the Colonel was on friendly terms. During the course of their conversation the young lady remarked coyly, 'With your extraordinary gifts did you never think of trying to become a really rich man?' The Colonel chuckled in reply, 'My dear girl, what do you know of riches? There are times when I think I am one of the richest men in the world! There is far more to riches than material possessions.' Equally, the Colonel could be extremely incisive. He was invited by the Duke of Hamilton in 1942 to deliver an address on the qualities of leadership, at a conference of officers. At one stage in the seminar the discussion centred on the definition of 'morale.' The discussion lasted all morning and every officer present expounded his conception of 'morale' at considerable length. Just before the Colonel (who was an invited speaker) rose to deliver his talk, the chairman unexpectedly asked if he would care to define 'morale' before starting his address. There was a short silence. 'Morale?' said the Colonel, 'Why — morale is but the mastery of oneself.'

6

The Sabreur

Throughout his life Colonel Campbell was fascinated by the art of fencing and was himself proficient both in theory and in practice. He was responsible for forming the Edinburgh University Fencing Club and set the pattern for the development of fencing in the University where, during the 1939-45 war, after the Salle Crosnier had closed down, he kept warm the embers of Scottish fencing. He held Crosnier in high regard. 'When Crosnier attacks,' he said, 'it is like trying to parry a streak of light, but when I attack Crosnier my blade seems trapped in a cage.' The very existence of the Salle d'Armes in the Pollock Institute is due to Colonel Campbell's foresight.

Such was his keenness on the moral value of fencing that even after his retirement in 1946 he plodded round in the evenings, carrying a heavy fencing bag, to teach in church halls and other places where he had managed to spark off some interest in the art. He fenced his last competitive match with success at the age of seventy, and thereafter continued presiding. One night around 11.00 p.m. at the house of Colonel Daniel Mackenzie, all the drawing-room furniture was pushed against the wall, out came the masks and sabres and he gave as good a lesson as any Master-at-Arms. Colonel Campbell even carried on his experiments during his last competitive match, carefully analysing the reactions of a man of seventy compared with the brilliant upcoming fencers in their twenties. He reckoned that he won his points by 'generalship' — the triumph of experience over vigour.

He was an honorary member of the Epée Club at the unanimous invitation of its committee and served as an elected committee member of the Amateur Fencing Association from 1919 until 1929. He was a Vice-President of the Scottish Amateur Fencing Union from 1934 to 1939 and President from 1948 to 1949 when the Union was reconstructed after the Second World War. Much is owed to his guidance during that difficult period.

Among his fencing achievements was the distinction of being one of the four British sabreurs who in 1913 reached the final of an International Tournament at Earl's Court. Fencing sabre, and sometimes also epée, he competed in Military Tournaments in Paris in 1914, at the Hague and in Paris in 1922, and again in Paris the following year. Such was his élan that in one international match where the British competitor in the Epée had taken ill he took on the Hungarian European champion although he had never handled an epée prior to the contest. Before the match the Colonel approached the Hungarian at the end of a practice session. 'You have a most effective style,' he said, 'Is your success anything to do with the way in which you hold the epée?' 'Of course,' replied the Hungarian, delighted at the interest of the British performer. 'It matters a lot how the weapon is held — let me show you.' He then proceeded to show the Colonel exactly how he gripped his weapon! A most useful lesson which the Colonel used later to the best advantage.

At that time an Epée contest was decided by the first hit, which made competitors extremely wary before making a critical move and the opening gambits were usually of an exploratory nature. The Hungarian, of course, did not know that the Colonel had not fought epée before but on the other hand the Colonel was a skilled sabreur and a former boxing champion. By a combination of boxing footwork, and sabre techniques, he so mesmerised the Hungarian that the champion was held off for over ten minutes before moving in for the kill.

In 1920 Colonel Campbell fenced epée and sabre in the Olympic Games in Antwerp and in the same year was placed second equal, along with two others, in the British Amateur Sabre Championship. At the 1920 Olympic Games, he gave an early demonstration of the standards of sportsmanship which were to dominate British athletics for decades and which are still accepted by many, although now under attack. The fencing section of the Games was rapidly degenerating into an international squabble. Heated arguments constantly took place between competitors, judges and referees, and the atmosphere was thick with suspicion and mistrust. The spectators were irritated and the whole affair was getting out of hand. The British were drawn against the Americans and the match had scarcely started before competitors and officials had formed a gesticulating group in the middle of the arena. The crowd had had enough and uproar broke out in the stadium. It looked as if the session would be closed in disorder when the rugged Captain of the British team picked up the microphone, 'Ladies and Gentlemen,' he said, 'Don't be alarmed - we are not arguing. The British team and our friends the Yanks are upset at the rotten spirit in which these matches are being conducted; so we have agreed to dispense with the judges and acknowledge our own hits. The reason for the commotion is that the judges and referees have never seen this done before in an Olympic competition and were against the idea. However, they have been persuaded and you can see them now, going over to the side seats where they will join the spectators.' There was a sudden hush as the Colonel's quiet voice explained how the British and Americans intended to conduct their own elimination bouts, dispensing with all the referees and retaining only a judge to decide which hit was first in the event of both opponents simultaneously acknowledging. Thunderous applause greeted these remarks as the spectators settled down to enjoy the remaining bouts of the day.

The decision of the British and Americans to dispense with referees and acknowledge their own hits had a profound effect on the subsequent conduct of the fencing section of the Games. The contentious spirit evaporated and participants of all countries now vied with each other in demonstrating that they were good sportsmen. Some continentals even acknowledged hits that never were! Colonel Campbell had once again demonstrated that, given the right leadership, high qualities of personal conduct can be introduced at even the top levels of competitive excellency. The Colonel tells the story in an early volume of *The Journal of the Army Physical Training Corps*. In his usual generous way he gives the Americans credit for an idea which most certainly originated from himself.

'We first met him at Antwerp, far from his native heath. It was during the Olympic Games. The Fencing was in progress, but the judging wasn't: that never seemed to progress. Between every phrase there was a prolonged and heated argument, which led to nothing. "Say, Britisher, let us fight it out alone, acknowledge our hits, and settle this affair; these guys make me tired." "Right-o," said the Britisher. Britisher and Yank fought it out, acknowledged their hits, and settled the bout in three minutes. The astonished judges watched in amazement. It was their first lesson in Sport. That was the beginning of the discovery of the American. "Come to our country, Britisher, and fight us for a trophy which we will give!" "Right-o," said the Britisher.'

Colonel Campbell was placed third in the British Amateur Sabre Championships in 1926 and became British Champion in 1929 at the age of 51. In the final pool every other competitor was young enough to be his son. He was also running a temperature which may have speeded up his reactions. He captained a British team against the United States of America in New York in 1921, himself fencing sabre, and this led to his being made Honorary Captain of the U.S.A. team which fenced in London in 1930. For Scotland he fenced sabre against England in 1929; against a U.S.A. team in Edinburgh in 1930; and against England in London in 1930 and 1934, captaining the team on some of these occasions.

The tournaments at the Hague in 1922 and in Paris in 1923 were in both cases the Military Epée and Sabre Championships of Europe. Colonel Campbell himself selected and led the British Inter-Services teams for these events. In 1922, as no public funds were available for fares, the Netherlands' invitation had at first been declined by the War Office; but at The Hague, British officers who had competed ten years earlier were still warmly remembered even by name, and the hosts informed the British Military Attaché that if the British team with its infectious sportsmanship did not come, there would be such discord that they would regret holding the Championships. To save the situation, the team members paid their own fare and found the Championships a most friendly event, an especially happy and close match being fenced against the Danes. In order to illustrate true qualities of sportsmanship, the British and the Danes at the Colonel's suggestion dispensed with the usual array of judges and acknowledged their own 'hits.' Neither side, to the amazement of the other teams, knew which team had won until the scorer had been consulted.

'Fencing,' said Colonel Campbell, 'is a physical exercise that develops sportsmanship, courage, determination to win, endurance, generalship and the team spirit. It also quickens the mind's powers of observation and reasoning.' He would illustrate his talks by drawing triangles bearing the above attributes building up the sides of a pyramid, each pair giving birth to a higher quality until at the apex was found: 'leadership.'

In one of his last illustrations, drawn about 1949, Colonel Campbell has carefully assessed the relationship between physical, mental and moral attributes as —

> Moral to mental — 5 to 3
> Mental to physical — 3 to 1
> Moral to physical — 5 to 1

Clearly as the years went by he was placing more emphasis on the moral and mental attitudes that underlay all physical activity.

In his own fencing Colonel Campbell always studied the mind of his opponent, while watching also his technique. He worked hard at his fencing, thinking out unusual strokes and practising them by himself tens of thousands of times before executing them in action. He was most scrupulous to acknowledge the slightest touch — otherwise, perhaps, he would have won the Championships earlier than he did. Campbell was keen on the acknowledgement of 'hits' not only in fencing but in all sport. He maintained that players of all games should acknowledge immediately and with good grace, adverse scores, and applaud the scorer on the other side. The current all too common view that what the referee doesn't see doesn't matter was anathema to him. 'Games,' he said, 'are not intended as sublimated duels — but are a means of fostering good will and understanding among spectator and participant alike. This is the essence of amateur sportsmanship.'

7

The Scottish Association of Boys Clubs

The S.A.B.C. invited Colonel Campbell to their annual conference in 1929. By that time the officebearers were aware that he might settle permanently in Scotland. His work with the National Association was already well known and he was welcomed enthusiastically by the Scottish Clubmen. Inevitably he was appointed a vice chairman of the Scottish Association and held that office until 1943.

As vice chairman he quickly associated himself with leaders and members throughout the country. He continued to emphasise that clubs existed not merely to provide activities for boys, but to help boys develop their complete personality — physically, mentally and morally.

Those ideals found a ready response from many of the men then associated with the Scottish Boys' Club movement. Those were the great days of the movement in Scotland. W. Hewitson (Nunky) Brown, Stanley Nairne, Jack Tait, Ronald Selby Wright, and W. Grierson MacMillan were just some the outstanding Scottish leaders who were closely involved with Ronnie Campbell and his ideas.

The Colonel was at home in such company. Some he already knew personally. 'Nunky' Brown had been present, along with Colonel Campbell, during the Toynbee Hotel Conference in 1923, when the historic decision to form the N.A.B.C. was taken. Stanley Nairne had founded the North Merchiston Club in Watson Crescent, Edinburgh, in 1921 and devoted his life to the Club until 1968. Jack Tait was another leader associated with the North Merchiston Club. He became the General Secretary of the Scottish Association in 1956. The Very Reverend Dr R. Selby Wright founded the Canongate Boys' Club and was to become a nationally known figure and Moderator of the General Assembly. W. Grierson MacMillan was another stalwart who was Secretary of the Edinburgh Academy Stockbridge Boys Club for many years. He was President of the Edinburgh Union from 1969 to 1973. As a group they shared the same high ideals as their English counterparts and gave themselves to the movement in the same dedicated way.

Campbell was usually present at the S.A.B.C. Annual Conferences which were held in Bonskeid in Perthshire. Every free moment he was out bird watching with a number of leaders. He told wonderful tales about birds and could answer their calls in a realistic way. It was his

96

custom on Saturday afternoons to lead a party to look for Capercailzies' nests. This was one of the highlights of the Conference. The expeditions through woods and hills were long and arduous, but there was never an occasion when the party did not report having found at least one nest. Many leaders in the movement who are now keen bird watchers owe their abilities to Colonel Campbell's leadership and inspiration. At the impromptu concerts on Saturday evenings Ronnie Campbell was one of the star turns. He would tell of his experiences in East London and imitate the cockney speech of the lads with whom he had worked. He also imitated the calls and actions of birds and animals in a most comical way.

But Colonel Campbell's main work with the S.A.B.C. was to introudce leaders and boys to new methods of physical recreation. He visited clubs in all parts of Scotland and advised them in such activities as boxing, fencing and gymnastics. As a result there was an increased interest in these activities.

One of Campbell's most enthusiastic Edinburgh supporters was 'Willie' Bell who was the leading physical training instructor in the North Merchiston Club. Willie Bell was an 'old boy' of the Club and an enthusiast for physical fitness and outdoor activities. In co-operation with Willie Bell, Colonel Campbell arranged for leaders training courses to be held in the North Merchiston Club. Here he experimented with many of his ideas and encouraged leaders of other Boys Clubs in Edinburgh to adopt them, and also to invent their own training schemes.

At the Edinburgh University Gymnasium, with club leaders and boys, he worked out a programme of activities whereby boys were able to test their skills against certain standards. This was the forerunner of the physical tests now operated by the National Association of Boys' Clubs and the Duke of Edinburgh's Award Scheme. Under Colonel Campbell's direction new interest was aroused in physical activities and the type of training he advocated is the pattern still used in many Scottish Boys' Clubs.

Boxing had been a major activity in the London Federation but the Colonel's efforts to promote the art in Scotland were not very successful. He found that some of the boxing in the Edinburgh Boys' Clubs had become mixed up with professionalism and felt that the spirit of boxing in those clubs was not conducive to the right ideals. 'Attitudes' were most important and the Colonel was not afraid to speak plainly. He was extremely critical of clubs where he found poor leadership. He scathingly described clubs where boys played snooker in a smoke filled room as 'opium dens.'

During his years in Edinburgh he was as much involved in the work of the S.A.B.C. as he had been in the London Clubs and the National Association. As a result the Scottish Movement was greatly enriched.

8

A Boy Scout at Heart

Colonel Campbell was a close friend of Lord Baden-Powell and took a keen interest in the Boy Scout movement. He was attracted by what he called its 'moral basis.' It is possibly a historical accident that on retiral from the Army he identified himself with the Boys' Club movement rather than with the Boy Scouts. At the time, the Boys' Clubs offered greater opportunities for full time service, and it so happened that he had that he had close personal links with many of the London Federation men.

When the Colonel first met Baden-Powell is not known with certainty. His family believe that Baden-Powell consulted the Colonel prior to compiling the exercises in *Scouting for Boys*. The first edition was published in 1908 which would date the friendship back to the early 1900s. Baden-Powell was appointed Inspector General of Cavalry at Home in 1903 and held that post until 1907 when he retired from the Army to form the Boy Scout movement. As early as 1906 B.P. sent an outline of his scheme of *Scouting for Boys* to the leading members of boys' movements as well as to important personalities in the Army, the Navy, the Church and the State. By then Campbell was well-known in England as an outstanding sportsman. Although he was a junior officer it is more than likely that he was consulted among others either directly or indirectly on those aspects of the new movement which involved physical recreation.

During the Great War, the Boy Scouts did their bit by guarding telephone lines and bridges and by acting as messengers, orderlies and despatch runners at the headquarters of the Chief Commanders. Colonel Campbell was out of the country during much of this period but obtained a first hand impression of the effectiveness of the movement while employed at Southern Command after his injury during the early months of the war.

We are on sound ground however by 1918 when Colonel Campbell took over the Inspectorship of the Army School of Physical Training. By that time he had emerged as a national war hero of senior army rank. During the same period Baden-Powell took up residence at Pax Hill, near Farnham, Surrey where he lived until his retirement to Kenya in 1939. While the Colonel was at Aldershot he often visited Baden-Powell at Pax

Hill, only a few miles away, and Baden-Powell attended the Colonel's demonstrations at Aldershot and gave talks to the troops.

The Scout movement had now grown into a major world force and the founder was turning his attention to an organisation for the older boy — the Rover Scouts. This was an idea dear to the Colonel's heart, and it was only natural that B.P. asked his advice both in connection with *Rovering to Success* published in 1922 and also about the formation of the Rover Scout movement itself. *Rovering to Success* ran into 26 editions, the last being published in 1964. The book contains no acknowledgements. Baden Powell consulted many outstanding men in connection with the formation of both the Boy Scouts and the Rover Scouts so it is impossible to ascertain from the book itself the part played in its compilation by Colonel Campbell. By the early 1920s, Colonel Campbell was not simply a well-known sportsman and naturalist as he was in 1908, but a nationally known war hero with immense experience. His influence on Baden-Powell must surely have been much greater than in his earlier years. Only at one point in the book, however, does the Chief Scout make even an indirect reference to the Colonel and that is where he refers to a 'troup of gymnastic instructors at the gymnasium at Aldershot.'

The text, however, refers to many matters on which the Colonel placed great emphasis. It elaborates important attributes of character such as reverence, self-expression, self-control and chivalry, and lays specific emphasis on service to the community — of which the Colonel was a life-long advocate. Curiously enough the book also contains schedules of a type which the Colonel often used to illustrate his own theories. It is impossible now to isolate the influence of Colonel Campbell on the formation of the Rover Scouts but the probabilities are that it must have been considerable.

As the years passed, the friendship matured and the two men kept in touch until B.P.'s death in January 1941. Throughout the entire relationship the minds of both men were enriched by the exchange of ideas and the Colonel readily acknowledged his debt to the Chief Scout.

'Baden-Powell made us realise,' he wrote, 'that what matters in training and makes it worthwile, is its moral value, and its power to create spirit by developing the qualities that make for character. At the same time he made it clear that those qualities can only be won by constant self-effort and guts.'

The Chief Scout and Colonel Campbell had much in common. An Army background, a love of nature, an awareness of what makes a boy tick, a gift of story-telling, an insight into the attributes of character, and a belief in voluntary service to the community.

Despite the Colonel's tremendous work for the Boys' Clubs he still found time to play an active part in the Boy Scouts. Many aspects of scouting appealed to the Colonel and the origin of some of his ideas can readily be traced in *Scouting for Boys*. The Chief Scout placed considerable emphasis on such aspects of character as chivalry, unselfishness, self-sacrifice, cleanliness, generosity, and illustrates these virtues vividly in *Scouting for Boys*. Most of them are included in the Colonel's schedule of attributes compiled during his later university years.

It was the moral basis of the Boy Scouts that inspired much of the Colonel's contribution to the 'Principles & Aims of the Boys Club Movement.' He knew from experience that, to be effective, a youth organisation needed an underlying faith and purpose. Without moral inspiration even the best of clubs simply wither away. Unless club leaders have a clearly defined sense of ultimate purposes the Colonel reckoned that they are probably doing more harm than good.

The Colonel saw the Boy Scouts as starting with a moral objective and then training the boy to achieving that objective, whereas the Club movement often started activities to interest the boy without having given sufficient thought to the eventual outcome of such activities. This philosophic distinction between the two movements never ceased to concern the Colonel and in his work with the Boys Club movement he constantly tried to give it what he called 'moral direction.'

Colonel Campbell was particularly attracted to a movement which broke down national and religious barriers. Shortly after the Great War, he had been present when four troops of Boy Scouts marched out of a town in the Middle East and camped together in the desert. There were Christians, Jews, Muslems and Hindus in the party. The event made a lasting impression. 'A movement which can bring together for a common purpose boys so widely divided by religion and race, has my wholehearted support,' he said afterwards.

Colonel Campbell was a man of quiet Christian faith. Occasionally in discussion he would suggest that one of the best ways to ensure effective prayer was to associate prayer with physical action. 'We should do our exercises in the morning,' he taught, 'at the same time as we say our prayers.'

The Colonel practised what he preached. Throughout his life he rose early in the morning to carry through his routine of prayer and exercise — and would often repeat the pattern at night.

'Don't laugh at the idea of prayer and exercise being wrapped up together,' he once told a sceptic, 'believe me — there is nothing more certain than that the "word becomes flesh" — to quote the Old Book. Just think of the Nazi movement in Germany. The Nazis placed great emphasis on physical fitness but, as the young bodies were trained, evil thoughts were injected into the mind. As a result, Nazi Germany produced a generation of men whose whole being was evil.' 'By contrast,' he continued, 'if you direct the mind into noble thoughts as the body is strengthened you create men of noble character. That is the basis of the ancient code of chivalry.'

The Colonel's views on the association of exercise with prayer was clearly influenced by Baden-Powell's 'Six Exercises for Health' in *Scouting for Boys.*

'While carrying out the stomach exercises,' writes B.P., 'count aloud the number of the swing or what is better, thinking of it as part of your morning prayer with God, say aloud, 'Bless Tim,' 'Bless father,' and any of your family or friends in turn.'

The emphasis placed by the Boy Scouts on character development through physical training and natural outdoor pursuits was very much in line with the Colonel's own thinking on those matters. His original ideas on physical training as related to the Boy Scouts are embodied in a book, *Recreational Training for Scouts*, published in 1949. The then Chief Scout, Lord Rowallan writes in the Foreword that the book is a 'must' for every troop library and a standby for every pack or troop night, helping to build healthier, brighter, and happier boys, fit to enjoy life to the full and to make the world a better place for other people too.

In his introduction the Colonel hammers away at his life-long theme: 'In your training,' he says, 'think of the body as the factory of the soul ...' 'What chiefly matters is the thought which inspires the movement, and the effort of will with which it is performed. The habit of associating thought with action makes for character. What is character? It is a combination of moral qualities which have the power to express themselves. Character is dynamic and not a storehouse of static ideals. Character is manifest in action; it must be built up by acts, brick by brick; the finer and greater the number of acts the larger and more noble the benefits. As B.P. tells us, ally each exercise with character. In your training let each exercise be associated with an ideal you want to attain; associate it with an act of will ...'

Colonel Campbell was honorary adviser for recreational training to Scottish Headquarters of the Boy Scouts for twenty years and was at one time a District Commissioner for North Argyll. In his active years he travelled widely throughout Scotland on behalf of the Scouts, demonstrating his exercises at conferences and meetings of scouters. He organised sports and other activities at the Scottish International Jamboree at Blair Atholl. He frequently gave talks to Scout organisations on ornithology and he was a regular contributor of articles to *The Scottish Scout.* Colonel Campbell kept up his interest in Scouts and in 1945, when nearly 70, he again demonstrated the perennial quality of his youth by undergoing the 'Wood Badge' course at Gilwell.

In the last years of his life, partially blind, crippled and with his memory sadly impaired, he wore his scout neckerchief neatly knotted round his throat every day. To the end, he was a Boy Scout at heart.

9

Wider Interests

OLD WARRIORS

Colonel Campbell did not regard the gym as being exclusively for students. His vision went far beyond the confines of the University. Each Thursday evening he conducted his own 'Old Warriors' class where some of the members were over seventy years of age. This class was made up of University staff and volunteers from local shops, business and offices.

One stormy Thursday evening in November, the Colonel looked out from his house at 54a George Square and decided that only an idiot would go down to the gym on such a night. It was a chance to spend a comfortable evening at home. Then he thought of the disappointment it would cause if even one member of the class turned up and found the leader absent. So he wrapped himself up and plodded through the sleet and rain along Nicolson Street and down Drummond Street to the Pollock Gym. Inside he found sixteen of his 'Old Warriors' happily bouncing balls, throwing sticks and performing their exercises. This incident was often afterwards used to illustrate the principle that a leader must never let his side down.

There was scarcely an evening when some club, or troop of scouts was not in the gym. Colonel Campbell even taught blind boys to fence during these evening sessions. He had the contestants stand on a raised centre line, which gave them direction, with bells attached to arms and legs. Technique was limited because blades had to be kept constantly engaged to enable the boys to judge distance. In addition he frequently arranged family classes which he also conducted himself. Those were great fun with fathers, mothers and children all performing with gusto under his personal supervision.

The tremendous growth in the number of students and the consequent pressure on the gym resources have now made such contacts with outside bodies more difficult but the tradition of helping non-university organisations and particularly groups of blind, paraplegic and other handicapped people still continues.

EXPERIMENTS IN INDUSTRIAL WELFARE

During his years at the University, Colonel Campbell experimented with physical education as related to industrial welfare. He maintained that many accidents in industry are caused by what he described as 'footless-ness and handlessness.' To combat this he introduced research into the lifting and carrying objects of all descriptions, i.e. boxes, sacks, parcels and pipes. The Colonel's interest in the scientific handling of heavy loads dated back to his Canadian experiences. Prospectors had to carry large loads over long distances, and warehouse workers manhandled sacks weighing two hundred pounds. A photograph in the Museum of the Army Physical Training Corps at Aldershot shows a number of the Colonel's instructors on the Western Front, including Jimmy Driscoll, carrying vital pieces of equipment up the lines by means of the 'Yukon Pack.'

The dynamics of manual load-handling fascinated the Colonel and by the University period he had developed the technique into a highly scientific and very practical art. Porters from the Waverley Station were even brought into the gym to teach the Colonel's Staff the most expert way of handling packages of various shapes and sizes. His experiments were recognised far afield and industrial concerns often asked Colonel Campbell's advice on minimising accidents and increasing manual skills.

Special exercises were devised to meet specific problems and with highly successful results. Demonstrations were given at the request of among others - Cadbury, I.C.I., Mather & Platt, Manchester, as well as industrial welfare and safety societies. Systems of training devised by Colonel Campbell were introduced at Cadbury, Mather & Platt, I.C.I., and Newton Chambers of Sheffield.

The effectiveness of Campbell's approach to industrial problems was increasingly recognised just before and during the second World War. Demands for his services flooded into the University and demonstrations were organised in industrial centres at Birmingham, Manchester, Sheffield and Huddersfield by firms anxious that others might share the advantages that they had obtained from his advice. He responded generously to those invitations. Without payment, and in his own free time, he inspected factories, demonstrated his methods, and directed the training of leaders and supervisors.

As news of his success spread even wider, enquiries poured in from as far afield as India, and the volume of work became so great that he could scarcely cope. He was invited to expound his views through addresses, papers, and demonstrations at such conferences as that of the Industrial Welfare Society at Balliol College, Oxford, where he contributed a paper on 'Physical Education in Relation to Industry.' He also addressed the Royal Society for the Prevention of Accidents at its Annual Conference in the Caxton Hall, London; the International Students' Society at Zurich; and the Public Health Congress and the British Association. He contributed a paper on Physical Education, in 1954, at the first British

Commonwealth and Empire Conference of Physical Educationalists in Vancouver.

The effort which Colonel Campbell put into his industrial courses may best be illustrated by describing in greater detail his work at Newton Chambers, Thorncliffe, Sheffield. He first went to the works at Thorncliffe in January, 1944 to discuss with the directors the possibility of introducing 'physical training with a purpose.' As a result of this meeting, an ex-army physical training instructor, Alan Hewling, who had just joined the staff of Newton Chambers, came to the University gym in Edinburgh on a month's course designed by Campbell with special reference to industry.

In August 1944, a new training centre was opened at Thorncliffe at which apprentices, as part of their general training, were given an hour each day of Colonel Campbell's system of industrial physical training. A large measure of success was achieved. In a short time the boys found that, as well as being able to get rid of surplus energy, their hand and eye co-ordination had improved. They became more agile, their reflexes quickened and they experienced a better sense of equilibrium. Later, the course became more advanced, with special emphasis on ambidexterity, strength, agility and balance.

There was a two-way follow-up to the scheme. Alan Hewling made regular visits to Edinburgh, and Colonel Campbell made repeated visits to Thorncliffe. This gave them opportunities to exchange ideas and thus techniques were improved.

In 1951, and at the age of 73, the Colonel gave a talk at a conference at Boston, England, accompanied by a demonstration by the Newton Chambers apprentices, organised by Alan Hewling. Colonel Campbell did not visit Thorncliffe again but maintained a close connection by correspondence as long as he was able to write.

The industrial physical training course at Thorncliffe was carried on until 1965 when the gymnasium was required for adaptation as a training workshop. The management, however, are under no doubt that the Campbell physical recreation courses under the direction of Alan Hewling were of great benefit to many hundreds of young men during the twenty years that the scheme was in operation.

Colonel Campbell's training system made an immediate appeal to industrialists for a variety of reasons. No elaborate apparatus was required. The exercises had purpose and increased physical efficiency. The system helped to assess the aptitudes of young people for particular jobs. The training was directed towards awakening the senses, stimulating the mind, and increasing mental alertness and executive ability. Finally the training was carried out in a happy spirit which made for joy in effort.

Colonel Lelean recalls Colonel Campbell's opinion about the problem, 'that as much as eighty per cent of industrial unrest might be due to lack of healthy stimulus to activity which characterises those who find in their work a means of congenial self-expression.'
In short, Campbell believed that many industrial workers were 'misfits' or 'square pegs in round holes.' He contended, therefore, that physical and mental education should proceed together throughout school life. School leavers should be tentatively allotted to one of the two main groups of the industrial team, i.e. those who have special aptitudes for working with the hands and those who are better 'pushing a pen,' so that their further training could be suitably specialised and the natural leaders discovered and developed.

'At an early stage,' said Campbell, 'the utmost efforts should be made to fit the worker to the job and the job to the worker by vocational choice, vocational selection, industrial adaptation and applied psychology. Those engaged in industry should be helped to keep physically fit by games and recreative exercises, and the maximum use should be made of trained voluntary workers.'

In devising industrial physical training schemes, Colonel Campbell encouraged competitions which called for leadership and team-spirit, particularly those which gave the less proficient a chance of making as important a contribution as the expert. He also advocated that physical proficiency tests in a gymnasium should be an integral part of the training. He illustrated aptly from the football team the different kinds of training required for forwards and backs respectively but the identical team-spirit which united the individual players of the successful side.

To those who never met Colonel Campbell his teaching on industrial training may sound somewhat paternalistic, but in practice it was never like that. He simply saw that many people were unhappy in their work and in his great-hearted way he set about trying to help them in the only way he knew. His efforts met with a large measure of success. Much of what he attempted in his experiments is now accepted as sound industrial psychology.

YOUTH WORK

While resident in Edinburgh Colonel Campbell took an interest in assisting youth groups in Edinburgh and its vicinity. No group was too small to assist or too inaccessible for him to visit. He was keen to encourage youth work in all its aspects and was particularly emphatic that young people must 'never be let down.' Whenever there was a request to organise a course or give a demonstration Ronald Campbell and his team were there. In church halls and club premises throughout the Edinburgh district, Colonel Campbell gave demonstrations, organised courses, and tried to find leaders. The High Street, Newington, Leith, Juniper Green, Fountainbridge and Forth in Lanarkshire are just a few of the districts where he was a familiar visitor during, and immediately after, the War. During 1948 and 1949, for example, he held weekly fencing classes for young people in St George's Church Youth Club; Newington and St Leonards' Church Youth Club; Dalmeny Street Church Youth Club; Hope Park and Buccleuch Congregational Young Peoples Fellowship; The Tron Church Youth Club and various companies of Boy Scouts. At the same time he conducted weekly fencing classes for Scouters.

Wherever he went he encouraged those who met him to put their backs into their work and achieve results which they once thought impossible. He was also involved with adult and youth work in the Edinburgh University Settlement which organised activities both at High School Yards in the Pleasance and in Prestonfield, which is a housing estate in the southern suburbs. In 1942 he was invited to join the Executive Committee of the Edinburgh University Settlement. This was on the recommendation of O. Tweedie Stoddart who was then the warden of the Settlement and who had come under the influence of the Colonel some years previously. He played a full part in Settlement life and took part in its recreational and social activities.

BORSTAL

Colonel Campbell's interest in Borstal was aroused when visiting local institutions during the years when he was Inspector of Physical Training at Aldershot. He was a personal friend of Sir Alexander Paterson, a Prison Commissioner who had a particular interest in Borstal reform. Sir Alex encouraged members of the Boys Club movement to enter the Borstal Service as a career. Before the Great War Sir Alex was associated with the Dockland Boys Clubs and the friendship between the two men ripened on the Western Front. Both had a special interest in the tough and difficult boy and were prepared to go to much trouble to help such boys to become valuable members of society.

At Sir Alex's invitation the Colonel spent some nights in a Borstal cell to find out for himself just exactly what the conditions were like. As a result of his experience he made recommendations for a more enlightened treatment of young offenders, some of which were put into practice.

In one Borstal the boys showed him the tree they could climb out by. He said: 'You know you shouldn't tell me that.' The boys replied: 'Garn, you won't split ...' and he didn't. It was after talking to some Borstal boys that one of them paid him what he regarded as the greatest compliment of his life. After listening in silence to what the Colonel had to say the boy said quietly: 'You look a mug - but you ain't one.'

THE NATIONAL PLAYING FIELDS ASSOCIATION

The provision of playing fields was another cause taken up by Colonel Campbell. He believed that through organised games a community could develop the basic virtues of co-operation, team-work and leadership particularly among its younger members and for that purpose playing fields, in some form, were essential. The matter was so close to the Colonel's heart that on retiral he offered to devote the remaining years of his life to the work of the National Playing Fields Association. He was a member of the Council of the Association from 1938 until his death in 1963. He was a member of the General Purposes Sub-Committee in 1938 and 1939, of the Executive Committee 1945 to 1948 and of the Grants Committee in 1945 and 1946.

10

Carfin Hall

A CALL TO NEW STEVENSTON

New Stevenston is not prepossessing — particularly in winter. It is situated on a rise above the surrounding Lanarkshire countryside and the east wind seems to find its way into every nook and cranny. The visitor yearns for the character of the historic town, or the couthy comfort of the traditional Scottish village. Apart from the Victorian mansion of Carfin Hall now in use as a community centre, there is practically nothing to suggest that it was here that Colonel Campbell and his students carried out a social experiment between 1937 and 1946. One looks in vain for the paddling pool opened by the Queen in 1937. Like some long lost Greek oracle only reeds and rushes mark the site. The floodlit playground and the foundations of the twin youth clubs have long since been buried under the heavy clay soil. Few now remember the allotments and rabbit hutches that supplied the local people with a steady supply of food during the Second World War.

Cold and dismal the place may be in winter but of poverty there is now no evidence. New factories are established in the Carfin Industrial Estate and there is no soulsearing unemployment. The children are well-clothed and play happily with their new bikes in the Carfin Hall policies. It is a far cry from the deprivation of the 1930s when Colonel Campbell first became involved with the local community.

New Stevenston is an industrial village situated about a mile and a half out of Motherwell and just south of the M8. Before the Second World War there was a good train service between Princes Street Station, Edinburgh (now closed) and Holytown Station, which still serves the New Stevenston and Carfin Hall district. At that time it was one of the worst areas of unemployment in central Scotland. Designated by the Government as a special area, the place bore grim evidence of the deprivation which followed the general strike when second and third generations had been idle all their lives. Children grew up in dire poverty, having seen neither their fathers nor their grandfathers in work. Carfin Hall and its policies provided virtually the only local amenities and before the Second World War housed a government sponsored community centre. The grounds provided facilities for tennis, bowling, bee keeping and a variety of outdoor games while recreation courses and a lively dramatic club functioned within the building. The baronial mansion house had been built by a Victorian industrialist. According to local legend the owner failed in business and had to decamp during the night to avoid his creditors. There were even those who claimed to have seen the unmade beds left by the occupants on their hasty departure.

In 1936 Colonel Campbell was invited to become a Director of the Centre. Before accepting office he paid a visit to New Stevenston. The day was bitterly cold and the desolation in the district so complete that he decided there and then that he had seen enough of this kind of hopelessness in East London and that he would refuse the appointment.

While waiting for the return train at Holytown Sation, four pinched faces peered out at him through one of the waiting room windows. He looked in and found a number of local children huddled together round the waiting-room fire, the only warmth available. They had no heating at home. Colonel Campbell was so shattered by this experience that he changed his mind, accepted the Directorship and decided that something had to be done.

ROYAL VISIT

He ran two Assaults at Arms in Edinburgh and raised about £80. In July 1937, he used this money to take a contingent of students to Carfin Hall. They were distrusted and misunderstood. The unemployed wanted work not sympathy. All kinds of well-meaning civil servants and social workers had tried to help in previous years and achieved nothing. However by hard work and goodwill the students finally broke down the opposition of the local unemployed and together they built a paddling pool in the grounds of Carfin Hall. The Colonel chose a paddling pool as the first project as he reckoned that the local residents would be interested in something which would benefit their children — and he was right. The pool was opened on 4th May 1937 by Her Majesty the Queen. Unfortunately, it was discovered at the last moment that the diameter of the pipe supplying the pool with water was too small for it to be filled before the Royal Party arrived. Disaster was avoided with the assistance of the Motherwell Fire Brigade. Their tenders just managed to fill the pool and slip away by one gate as the Royal party were entering by another!

The visit of George VI and Queen Elizabeth to New Stevenston and Carfin was a royal spectacular and their Majesties received a wonderful welcome at the Hall. The grounds were in apple pie order under the supervision of the groundsman, Mr McClintock, and the old mansion house looked glorious in the sun. Early in the proceedings Colonel and Mrs Campbell were presented to their Majesties and later at the paddling pool Colonel Campbell had the honour of himself presenting William Rankine and Charles Hunter, two local unemployed men who had taken a prominent part in Carfin Hall activities. They told their Majesties how the students and unemployed together had built the paddling pool. This was a great moment in Colonel Campbell's life. He said afterwards that the spotlight of public opinion had been focussed sharply on the cancer of unemployment. Charles Hunter, for example, never had a job since the Great War. Nor was there work for his grown up children.

At the end of the summer vacation, the students left Carfin Hall through flag-bedecked streets and the station had to be closed to keep out the crowds — surely an epic in student history.

The students had put Carfin Hall on the map. They had also gained the confidence of men who had not worked since the Great War. There were at that time over two million men out of work and it is difficult for young people today to appreciate the physical and moral degradation of long term unemployment on such a massive scale. The students found out what unemployment really meant. They saw the terrible effects of the dole system as it ate like dry rot into the fabric of society. They realised that the unemployed with whom they were working were forgotten men, without a future and without hope. They saw how the children were growing up with even less hope — malnourished, badly housed and underprivileged. One child took off eight dirty old jerseys in the Carfin Hall changing room on a broiling hot day. The child explained that his mother had insisted on his wearing the old jerseys so that the students would not notice his thin and underfed condition.

The following year the students and local unemployed built a floodlit concrete playground — the first of its kind in Scotland, and finally in 1939 the Government gave a grant of £7,000 for building premises for a Boys and Girls Club and large hall, with voluntary labour. This was an achievement of which Colonel Campbell was justly proud. He was certain that had it not been for the earlier work ultimately recognised by Royal patronage, Government support for the club project would not have been forthcoming. Once again a team of students under Colonel Campbell's leadership descended on Carfin Hall. The foundations were laid by voluntary labour in July and arrangements were made to have the building completed by contract during the autumn.

THE CARFIN HALL SOCIETY

On an evening during July 1939 with Colonel Campbell as chairman, the students founded the Carfin Hall Society. During the course of the discussion, Colonel Campbell asked everyone present to pledge themselves to work unceasingly for the unemployed and to endeavour to awaken public opinion to the plight of men without work.

Campbell suggested that those who believed in his ideals should act like leaven in the community to achieve acceptance of the public obligation to ensure that work is available for all. He contended that disciplined work is the bedrock of morality in every modern society and said so in no uncertain terms.

'We have drifted into a flabby habit of looking down on hard work and despising those who do it. This attitude is fundamentally wrong. Service expressed in labour is a worthy contribution to society.'

He discussed associated problems such as housing, health, hygiene and education. In particular Colonel Campbell maintained that the long term effects of unemployment benefit — the 'dole' as it was then called — was the disintegration of man's character. For that reason he advocated that payments by way of relief to the unemployed should be on a short term basis only. It was the duty of organised Government to ensure that all men were provided with work.

Ample leisure time for purposeful creative activities was an essential ingredient in Colonel Campbell's 'hard work' philosophy. The more uncongenial the job the greater the number of compensating leisure hours. With a twinkle in his eye Colonel Campbell suggested that everyone could do with six weeks holiday. This represents forty days in the wilderness and a day to get there and a day for the return journey. This of course was a counsel of perfection but clearly illustrates the Colonel's philosophy of hard work balanced by adequate recreational opportunities. Leisure time however was intended for purposeful use. Education for leisure was an essential ingredient in the Colonel's philosophy of work, and at least part of leisure time ought to be devoted to voluntary service in the community.

Colonel Campbell also urged the provision of more day nurseries. He felt that many women led drab and unfulfilled lives after the birth of their children. The nursery properly used could be a means of developing their creative talents and so benefit society as a whole. He did not want more nurseries simply to encourage mothers to go out to work. Nothing was further from his thoughts.

The Colonel designed the Society's badge — 'A dandelion breaking through concrete.' He chose the design because it was found in 1939 that dandelions were already forcing their way through the concrete of the playground laid only a year previously. Colonel Campbell took this as an object lesson. Nothing could stop the dandelion forcing its way to the sun. This was creative activity and hence the motif of the dandelion and the concrete.

THE MIRACLE OF CARFIN

Colonel Campbell was perturbed at the bitter Protestant - Roman Catholic relations which characterised the surrounding district. Until the autumn of 1920, Carfin had no wider fame that that of any other mining village on the Lanarkshire coalfield. That year however there was consecrated the Grotto of Carfin, a religious shrine venerated by the Roman Catholic Church. As the years wore on the waters of the Grotto became credited with miraculous powers and the shrine was regarded by thousands of Roman Catholics in Scotland with a reverence almost equal to that accorded to Lourdes. To many Protestants, however, it was a symbol of Popish authority flaunted in the Protestant face.

By 1937 the situation had become so bad that many neighbours had not been on speaking terms for years. Carfin Hall, however, soon became a communal meeting place and many Protestants and Roman Catholics found a new friendship within the team spirit of the projects there. Both minister and priest associated openly together in Colonel Campbell's activities.

Eventually Protestant and Catholic families who had been at each other's throats for years went along the road together on Sundays — one family to church, the other to chapel — and then waited for each other afterwards. The real 'Miracle of Carfin' took place unnoticed by the Scottish public or the Press.

'Racial or religious divisions cannot be healed by legislation or exhortation alone,' emphasised the Colonel during the course of a discussion. 'There must be joint participation in creative projects directed to the well being of the whole community. Only by working together can there be mutual appreciation of the distinctive gifts which each section of the community contributes for the benefit of the others.'

Such practical views are very apposite today when parts of our country are torn apart by religious and racial strife.

The outbreak of war in September 1939 brought the main work at Carfin Hall to an end. The buildings were never completed, but interest was maintained in the Community Centre for a long time afterwards. In the early days of the war the Army occupied the centre but as a result of representations by Colonel Campbell the Army vacated the premises which were used throughout the war for civilian welfare work.

Until the end of the war, students went regularly to the centre. They helped in digging allotments and running a rabbit farm as well as in sharing club work with young people. The warden during the whole period of Colonel Campbell's association with Carfin Hall was a Quaker, Mr Reid. Mr Reid was a quiet kindly man who worked well with the Colonel. Both Mr Reid and his wife, who ably assisted him, must have put up with a lot as armies of students tramped through their domain.

Between 1939 and 1945 local boys from the district of Carfin were taken by Colonel Campbell to his wartime work camps, of which more hereafter. After the war, prosperity returned to the district and the work of the Society ceased. For several years, however, the Society was extremely active and was represented by an official committee of the Students Representative Council which not only took a great interest in the work but also supported it financially.

11

The Second World War

When war broke out in 1939 Colonel Campbell was at once re-employed by the Army and for several months appeared in the University gym in military uniform. It was almost exactly four decades since he had enlisted in the Nelson Rifle Company. As he put on his uniform for the last time he had poignant memories; of the long march to Pretoria; of his Canadian comrades dead beside him at Paardeberg; of Mons, the Somme, Woodbine Willie, and Sergeant Wilcox; of depots and gymnasia throughout the world. Colonel Campbell was a practical man. He realised that his soldiering days were gone. From a man of war he had become a man of peace. At his own request he returned to civilian life where he felt at his age he could make a greater contribution to the war effort. However, he continued to serve in the Home Guard and Civil Defence. During the entire six years of war he quietly organised training courses for volunteers in southern and central Scotland.

Campbell realised instinctively that the coming conflict would be quite different from the Great War, particularly with regard to civilian participation. One of the most important national tasks would be to achieve self-sufficiency in food production and to that end he worked unsparingly throughout the next six years. Soon after the outbreak of war, he formed the Edinburgh University Allotment Association which cultivated twenty four allotments at the women's playing grounds at Peffermill until 1945.

Colonel Campbell took a leading part in the Association by maintaining his own allotment, encouraging students to 'Dig for Victory' and in arranging competitions and social activities for the allotment workers. He also, with his family's help, looked after an allotment in George Square Gardens along with another nearby in the Meadows, from which he supplied several households.

One of his main efforts, however, was in the clearing of Scottish hill land of bracken to increase the production of sheep. Bracken seems to have a special attraction for land otherwise good for timber or grazing sheep, and during the war the cultivation of marginal land became a critical factor in achieving self-sufficiency in food production. His bracken cutting campaigns were thus not without national significance.

'There are three curses of the Highlands,' he would say laughingly, 'the midges, the bracken and the Campbells.'

He certainly did his best to rid the country of bracken. Each year throughout the war, bracken-cutting camps were in action during the three months of the University summer vacation. They were held at places such as Connel Ferry and Strachur in the North, and Lamington and Dumfriesshire in the South. Vast hillsides were tackled by scythe and sickle. The trail blazers marked out with flags, the areas to be cut, and the work was tackled systematically by the volunteers, acre by acre — rain, storm or sunshine. Cutting started at 7 am and went on until at least 6 pm with an hour for lunch. In true Army fashion there was an additional break of ten minutes in every hour. Nowadays bracken can be sprayed by chemicals from a helicopter but those techniques had not been perfected by 1939. At that time the only sure way of getting rid of bracken was by regular hand-cutting.

The students were housed in huts, bothies, tents, outhouses and church halls. Lucky students were sometimes given hospitality in private houses. As well as work of national importance the camps provided an opportunity for country interests and pursuits. 'The healthy life in the country,' maintained the Colonel, 'the comradeship, the work, the wholesome food and recreation make the camps an excellent and natural course in physical training as well as a training in leadership.'

In order to make the camps self-supporting, local subsidiary camps were organised at Christmas and Easter to dig allotments and plant the vegetables which were later eaten during the summer. Apart from bracken-cutting, the camp workers took part in forestry and agriculture, including turnip singling, thistle cutting and haymaking. Many an agricultural worker must have stared in amazement at the 'gallant Colonel' as, headed by a piper, he led his men with shouldered scythes, sickles, or axes into the fields and forests at 7 am on a filthy morning. Not only did he lead his volunteers during the day, but equally did he lead the revels in the evening. He inspired all who worked with him — a born leader of men.

In addition to the physical objective of clearing land for sheep and in assisting agriculture and forestry, Colonel Campbell had wider purposes in running these camps. Almost always there were a number of boys from Carfin in the team. Some of these boys had never been in a train in their lives and their diet seemed to have been limited to bread, and fish and chips. Here was a rich field of social work in which both Colonel Campbell and his students became intimately involved.

'Country life gives these lads a chance to develop their personality,' the Colonel told his student leaders. 'It provides a natural means of training the senses and developing the powers of observation. By taking part in rural pursuits the mind is improved. Sympathy with nature is essential for our well being.' 'That's all very well,' grumbled some of the students, 'but the boys are a bit of a pest and some of them down right shirkers.' 'Quite right,' retorted the Colonel. 'That is why you are here. It is not easy to get boys to concentrate on a job for any length of time. They work in fits and starts and damage and mislay their tools. Your job is to teach them, and set an example. By the end of camp you will see a difference.'

The boys were always up to mischief and a continual source of concern to the students. Their leader was a lad called 'Shug' Robertson who, given a chance, would have excelled in any profession. Meat was short during the war years and one evening at Lamington the local rabbit catcher came into the camp carrying two snares which had been illegally set. The rabbit catcher complained to the Colonel and asked him to ensure that no one from his camp would engage in this kind of illegal practice. During the course of the evening meal, the Colonel asked if anybody present had been guilty of the misdemeanour. There was a stony silence. 'All right,' said the Colonel. 'I hope it was not one of you boys, but at any rate see that it never happens again.' The matter was almost immediately forgotten but that night 'Shug' was not in bed by 10 o'clock and could not be found.

That night most of the students were out with the Colonel scouring the countryside in an effort to find the missing boy, but without success. At 6 o'clock in the morning a tired 'Shug' trailed into the camp carrying over his arm some 20 snares. When tackled by the Colonel he replied belligerently, 'The rabbit catcher took my snares and now I have got all his.' This town-bred boy had scoured the countryside for miles around and somehow managed to pick up almost every snare laid by the rabbit catcher.

How the Colonel dealt with this domestic crisis is not altogether clear but those who were present believe that he quietly recompensed the rabbit catcher for the loss of the snares and his rabbits. Nothing more was said about the incident however, and 'Shug' left the rabbit catcher's snares alone in the future.

The 1941 summer camp at Lamington lasted for nine weeks. Lord Lamington was an old comrade of the Colonel's and the estate was thrown open to the work camp members. Most of the students were housed in the village hall for which the Colonel paid a weekly rent of fifteen shillings but some lodged in the Old Parsonage which was the home of Mr and Mrs McLehose of the well-known firm of Glasgow printers and publishers.

Cripple children from Challenger Lodge, Edinburgh, had been evacuated to Lamington House and were involved by the Colonel in the activities of the camp. The children were organised into parties who helped to weed and maintain the allotments which provided the camp with vegetables. They had a special plot of their own and staged their own fruit and vegetable show at the end of the summer. They were also encouraged to give concerts for the camp workers and villagers thus bringing the entire community in Lamington together. Thirty-seven men, women and boys took part in the Lamington camp during the summer of 1941. Among those who took part were the talented nephews of Jan Masaryk - Leonard and Herbert Revelloid. Their mother who was Jan Masaryk's sister had brought the boys from Czechoslovakia to the safety of Britain. Leonard joined the R.A.F. and was killed, while his young brother Herbert who was a brilliant violinist died a short time later.

In all his work the Colonel was well supported by leading students. At least three Senior Presidents of the S.R.C., as well as many other office-bearers and outstanding members of the athletic clubs took part in the work at Carfin Hall and the other work camps. The Colonel never wasted time and every rainy day provided an opportunity for a round table discussion at which plans for post-war rehabilitation were discussed. There was nothing 'airy fairy' about a Campbell discussion. Every worthwhile point was carefully written on a blackboard and then analysed at some subsequent meeting.

Colonel Campbell usually had his seminars on a Sunday which was regarded as a day of rest. He never asked his students to go to church with him, but set off for church himself about half-an-hour before the service began, usually followed by a motley crew of atheists, free thinkers and Christians of all denominations. In his more advanced years he sometimes fell asleep during the sermon but would be immediately awakened by his watchful companions.

Although political ideas were discussed during Colonel Campbell's seminars he was not a party man. It is doubtful whether anyone other than his most intimate associates knew his political affiliations - if indeed he had any. His nature and outlook were such that in the end he would be more likely to support the man rather than the party. On more that one occasion he said in no uncertain terms that he would vote against any government which was prepared to accept widespread unemployment as the price of economic progress. He mistrusted the dissimulation of politicians and he positively disliked civil servants whom he described as 'eating paper and having red ink in their veins.'

Colonel Campbell's work camps were well organised. He paid great attention to detail and kept a daily log of each student's output of work. He also prepared target objectives for each group as well as for the individual. His dictum that 'measurement is the basis of science,' would gladden the heart of the modern business manager. Each studen was expected to cut an acre of bracken each day, while a boy of 10 to 12 years old would cut half an acre. Some of the old records kept by the camp organisers make interesting reading. Turnip singling was paid by local farmers at the rate of sixpence for a hundred yards. A good student could earn a shilling in one hour's back-breaking work. Thistle cutting earned a man ten pence and a woman eight pence per hour.

Those who took part in the work camps were volunteers and received no pay. Colonel Campbell, however, either refunded the railway fare or issued a return ticket. In addition they were paid a small allowance each week which Campbell described as 'pocket money.' None of his students knew until long after Colonel Campbell had retired from University that the camps were largely financed out of his own modest resources, and that it was on him they had depended for underwriting the camp finances, and for their fares and pocket money.

After each camp those who had participated received a letter of thanks from the Colonel which usually had the effect of making the recipient think he had managed the whole camp singlehanded! Here again was a lesson in practical leadership. Colonel the Reverend Charles Scott Shaw of Adelaide, South Africa, who was a camp leader remembers this encouragement over thirty years later. 'Nor can I forget,' he writes, 'the way that good man always wrote me a personal note of thanks for my modest help in the organising of it. Colonel Campbell meant more to me than I can ever record.'

The fantastic vitality of the man was immediately apparent to those who took part in the camps. The Colonel rose early - about 5.30 - and liked to be on his own for the first half hour of the day. Alone with his thoughts he carefully went through his ritual of exercises. He then brewed up the 'gun fire' and brought a hot cup of tea to the early rising orderlies of the day. After breakfast he set off with the workers and usually spent a full day either cutting bracken on the hills or working in the forests or fields. After tea he worked until 9 o'clock in the allotments which provided vegetables for the camp or sat doing his desk work at an old table set in the middle of the dormitory. Occasionally, when bracken cutting was completed, he would set off round the nearby farms on an old bicycle trying to find farm work for the students. At Leamington there was a kindly farmer called Watson who seemed to go out of his way to help.

Colonel Campbell's desk work involved not only administration associated with the camp but also with other camps which he would be running at the same time. In addition he corresponded with the Department of Agriculture and other public bodies as well as with industrialists who were interested in his industrial courses.

From time to time he would disappear for the day to further some of his projects in Edinburgh or elsewhere or he would entertain some visiting 'big wig' with a view to enlisting support for his multifarious activities. And all this in a man approaching 70!

12

Salen and Acharacle

After the war the bracken camps ended, but Colonel Campbell transferred some of the work to Acharacle and Salen in Ardnamurchen, Argyll, where he had close pre-war associations.

During the autumn of 1921, the Colonel had become the tenant of Skipper's Cottage at Salen on Loch Sunart. That summer he had rowed over with the family from Movern and looked at the cottage which had been built by a South African millionaire for the captain of his yacht. Colonel Campbell subsequently bought the house which he kept until 1955. Niall Campbell was born there on 22nd September 1924. The Colonel was attracted to the district partly because its remoteness in those days offered scope for his interest in natural pursuits and also because of its proximity to the lands of Inverawe with which his family had been connected for generations. In some ways he was more at home in Argyllshire than anywhere else. He loved to get back to Salen where he felt at one with the people and their way of life.

When Colonel Campbell went to Salen the most convenient approach was by train to Glenfinnan and then by steamer down Loch Shiel, to Acharacle where three miles of road led to Salen. At that time the small steamer Clan Ranald plied daily between Glenfinnan and Acharacle. It was captained by Angus McDonald and a Gaelic-speaking crew of four. Captain McDonald was skipper of the boat for about forty years and died only recently. The Colonel liked his guests to travel in the Clan Ranald down Loch Shiel to Acharacle and then along the three miles of grassy road to his house at Salen. As the little steamer fussed along Loch Shiel it called at jetties which served isolated homesteads. The crofters would row out to the ship to pick up their mail and stores, or perhaps to convey sheep to some port of call further down the Loch, all the while passing the time of day in Gaelic.

A whole life style revolved round the lochside, the crofts, the steamer and the villages. Tourists were few and the roads unsuitable for motor cars. Communication was still largely by water. The community was closely knit and the ancient pattern of life based mainly on crofting still survived. All this has passed away. The steamer has gone long since. Only the launch owned by the public spirited proprietor of the Loch

Shiel Hotel plies its way in solitude between Glenfinnan and Acharacle. The lochside is deserted and is now the preserve of the Forestry Commission. The great mansion houses of Dorlin and Shiel Bridge have been demolished. The grass-grown roads have given way to well maintained tarmacadam surfaces which can scarcely cope with the endless summer flow of motor cars. Colourful worthies like 'Big John' and 'Old Andy' have gone to their last resting places. In the short space of twenty years a way of life so loved by Colonel Campbell has quietly disappeared.

In spite of a busy life, Colonel Campbell managed to take a great interest in Salen and the surrounding district, and also in Highland affairs. In this he was following in the footsteps of his father before him. From 1921 onwards the nature of his work enabled him to spend a number of months every year at Skipper's Cottage which became a second family home. The yearning to be close to nature was deep within him and in Argyll he found all that was necessary to re-charge him for his continual battles in the world outside.

At Easter he felled trees, sawed them up, and split them - enough for a whole year. He hated the smell, noise and uncertainty of outboard engines and would row in boats all day — fifteen to twenty miles with his family in the stern. During the 1920s with his wife and his young son Bruce, he 'circumnavigated' Loch Shiel, camping without a tent. Using the Colonel's backwoodsman's experience, the family either slept in the open or built leaf huts with growing trees as posts. Summers in Argyll, however, are not like the summers he knew in British Columbia and the following year the family bought a tent and camping became more conventional. When an old man, he built a leaf hut for his grand-children. It was smaller and more solid than those he had made on the shores of Loch Shiel and the doorway was crowned with a ram's skull. It weathered the gales of winter, and standing among bare trees and dead bracken, spoke eloquently of past skills and a life lived in harmony with natural things.

Whatever he did, sawing wood, rowing, walking or fishing, he quietly contemplated. The woods around Salen were his 'open air church.' He believed deeply in the direct contact of man with his Maker — aided by the peace and solitude of the wild countryside. In recognising man's need for periods of quiet and reflection, Colonel Campbell was in accord with the world's great philosophical and religious thinkers. But he expressed these ideas in such a commonsense way that they were easily understood by the most unimaginative of men.

Between the wars, along with his sister-in-law, Kitty Brockman, and others, he organised a successful Salen Arts and Crafts Society which held annual exhibitions which ceased on the outbreak of war.

He urged the need to provide work for crofters and small-holders during wet weather, for which Argyll is notorious. He experimented with the planting of willows, some types of which he believed could grow well on peat or poor soil. For years he sought to find a willow which would grow fast in the local soil and on which could be built up a local industry. Samples of willow trees were sent to Salen from all over the country, but he had to leave before this experiment could be completed. Colonel Campbell maintained that the Highlands would be difficult to repopulate unless reasonable recreational facilities were available.

He was, however, no starry-eyed idealist. He was totally opposed to any scheme which would increase the population of the Highlands beyond the capacity of the natural resources of the area. 'I believe,' he said, 'in a Highland economy which will support a comparatively small population at a high standard of living.'

As usual he translated his theories into action and shortly after taking up his house at Salen he began to build a playing field on a swamp littered with large boulders. He built the playing field largely with his own hands, assisted by anyone who could be 'press-ganged' into service, including his old friend Lt. Colonel Percy Honeyman, who was a regular visitor at Salen after 1928. Campbell had hoped that Colonel Honeyman might ultimately succeed him as Director of Physical Education and 'Honey's' untimely death in 1944 was a great shock to him. The digging, blasting, draining and levelling of the Salen playing field took twelve years and was complete by 1939. In his methodical way Colonal Campbell kept a record of every bucket and barrowload of material which was manhandled either out of or into the field. There must have been thousands of such operations.

He was particularly proud of the fact that early in the year hay could be grown in the field, thus making a contribution to local crofting. When the hay had been cut the field could then be used for children's games.

The field was taken over by the Army in 1939 and used for military exercises. After the war the War Office offered to remake the ground but a local farmer made a deal with the Colonel that in return for some Nissen huts which the Army had erected on the ground he would remake the ground. The farmer, however, did not keep the bargain and once again the Colonel buckled to. He remade the ground himself with occasional student help — and without one word of complaint or self-pity. When restored, the playing field reached a peak of popularity with a Children's Gala Day in 1949. The Sports were organised with great zest by Colonel Campbell a few weeks before his 71st birthday. After that, interest in the field declined and it has now reverted to its original marshy state. A recent inspection, however, suggests that with a little effort it could easily be restored to playing field standard.

Post war work in the Salen district was resumed in 1946 when Colonel

Campbell organised a work camp to build another playing field at Acharacle, three miles away on Loch Shiel. There on the outskirts of the village near the parish church on an impossible piece of uneven peat bog he started digging trenches preparatory to draining and levelling the ground. He chose the peat ground deliberately as he considered good land essential for growing crops. During the camp Colonel Campbell lived in nearby Shielbridge House (now demolished) while the students were accommodated in the stables, which still remain. The following year he organised a much larger camp at Acharacle under the direction of his former Chief Instructor Major Mather. He taught the volunteers the Boer War technique of tying twigs into bundles, styled 'fascines,' for use as bottoming for the ditches upon which the draining of the playing field depended. On this occasion Colonel Campbell stayed at Skipper's Cottage, visiting the site daily while the working party were lodged in Acharacle Village Hall. Over twenty five years later the ditches still run as true as ever although even local residents are now mostly unaware that the site marks an early post-war experiment in community relations.

By this time Colonel Campbell's strength was beginning to fail and the Acharacle project was never finished. Still he carried on. A team of students worked at Salen in 1948 restoring and finishing the Salen playing field. At the entrance there are two memorial stone gate pillars erected by the King George's Jubilee Trust. This was his last organised work camp, although individual students continued to work at Salen for a year or two afterwards. After the decline of the Salen playing field the memorial inscriptions were removed, but the pillars themselves still stand as a reminder of Colonel Campbell's many years of faithful service to the village of Salen and surrounding district.

13

'Aunty Pops'

No record of Colonel Campbell's work would be complete without reference to Mrs May Campbell, daughter of Colonel W. Brockman, whom he married in 1911. He had met her for the first time while on Army Service in Bermuda during 1908. In this so-called permissive age it is perhaps enough to say that they loved and supported each other for over half-a-century and celebrated their Golden Wedding at Bonskeid, Perthshire on 22nd April, 1961, together with their children and grandchildren and a number of life-long friends.

There are two sons of the marriage, both devoted to the open air and both professionally engaged in nature work. Bruce, the elder, for many years Secretary of the British Trust for Ornithology and later Senior Producer of the BBC's Natural History Unit, is now a writer and broadcaster on natural history and conservation as well as a consultant and editorial adviser on those subjects to *The Countryman* magazine. Niall, the younger, is the Regional Officer for North and West Scotland with the Nature Conservancy Council of the Department of the Environment.

Mrs Campbell was a true daughter of the regiment, skilled in the discipline of moving house and maintaining a well-organised ménage on a tight budget — gifts which were to be put to good use throughout her entire life. 'Aunty Pops,' as Mrs Campbell was affectionately called was a character in her own right and an ideal complement to her husband. The nickname 'Aunty Pops' arose from a fancied resemblance between her and the picture of a girl in a field of poppies. The Colonel called her 'Pops' or 'Poppers.' Mrs Campbell was English which gave rise to many quiet family jokes. When the children were young, the Colonel was teasing one of them about his mother's country of origin. 'Don't worry, daddy,' the boy rejoined, 'we'll pull mummy through.'

Mrs Campbell was blessed with a radiant personality and gave unstinting assistance to the Colonel who was for ever involved with people in difficulty. Her visits had a tonic effect on those she met. She had a sensitive perception of a person's needs and the gift of helping in a most practical way. She was a remarkable entertainer and an active sportswoman. Her vivacity and sense of fun had a magnetic attraction for young people.

She had a wifely insight into her husband's character and would recount stories that the Colonel would have preferred to forget. There was one which recalled a time in the early years of their marriage when the Colonel was working on a theory that if a man did the right exercises he could stand exposure for several hours without proper protection, even in arctic conditions. In order to test his theory he took his wife and young Bruce, then aged about seven, early on a cold spring day, on a picnic to the top of Ben Cruachan. There, in a freezing half gale, he took off nearly all his clothes and ran round the hill from early morning to late afternoon. 'There was I,' said Mrs Campbell, 'huddled on the freezing hilltop with little Bruce, trying to convince him that this silly man prancing round the top of the mountain in his underpants was really a genius working out a theory of great benefit to mankind.'

Dr R.E. Verney met the Colonel and Mrs Campbell on a Sunday afternoon at the Braid Hills Hotel in Edinburgh where the Campbells were entertaining four students who were the first residents in Cowan House - a University hostel in George Square, now demolished. The students were so impressed by the Colonel and his wife that they immediately got up a petition to the University requesting that the Colonel should be made warden of Cowan House. Nothing came of this suggestion and shortly afterwards Colonel and Mrs Campbell took possession of their flat above the Women's Union at 54a George Square, which at once became a mecca for both men and women students.

There was an Australian student in the early thirties who qualified in medicine with the minimum of finance. The Colonel nicknamed him 'Digger.' Mrs Campbell made sure that he dined once every week at 54a to make sure that he got at least one square meal every seven days. There must have been a large number of students who were quietly helped by Mrs Campbell in such practical ways.

During the next two decades a continual stream of needy and lonely undergraduates found their way to the same door. Not only were they given material help but they were received by Mrs Campbell with hospitality and charm.

The highlight of the week was Sunday afternoon tea at '54' when the drawingroom packed with students, resounded to gales of laughter at the Colonel's jokes and reminiscences. While the Colonel held the floor, Mrs Campbell moved quietly round the company, every now and then taking aside the student in need of special help or encouragement. She was backed up by Lizzie, a Midlothian girl who served the family for many years and who is now in retirement. Lizzie said little and usually worked in the background. She well knew the unlimited capacity of hungry students and seemed to conjure an almost endless supply of very welcome tea, scones, jam and cakes.

During vacations Mrs Campbell frequently participated in her husband's work camps, usually as cook or in general administration. She had tremendous energy and even in later years took part like a youngster in camps and picnics — on land or in water! Her patience must have been sorely tried at times by the constant stream of burly students who thumped through the flat in George Square, or by the turmoil which ensued when the Colonel gave impromptu fencing lessons in the drawing room.

While the Colonel was Director of Physical Education, Mrs Campbell played an active part in University life, and was also involved in all kinds of social work in the city. She was as well known as her husband and greatly loved. From the time of her husband's appointment, Mrs Campbell 'adopted' the Women's Athletic Club acting as an Honorary Member, and as Honorary President from 1937 to 1946. She had personal contact with each section, making tea in the pavilion, and sewing curtains and furnishings for the primitive changing rooms which existed at that time. She was a friend to many women especially lonely girls from abroad. Much of her work centred on the Women's Union where she served on the Committee of Management. At the Annual General Meeting of the E.U.W.A.C. held during 1946 fitting tribute was paid to her work since the early 1930s. At a farewell party held later that year she was presented with a brooch by the Club's President, Miss Helen Burns.

14

The Last Years

On retiral from the University in 1946, Colonel Campbell achieved the unique distinction of being awarded an honorary blue by the Athletic Club — an honour of which he was extremely proud. An appeal to mark his service to the University was arranged. Tom Houston and the Colonel's secretary, Mrs Simpson, obtained access to the University records and a letter was sent to every graduate who had been associated with the Athletic Club since the Colonel's appointment. The response was phenomenal. For weeks a torrent of envelopes containing cheques and cash poured in to the appeals office from all over the world. The presentation was made by the Rector, Sir Donald Pollock, in the fencing salle at the Pollock gym. After speaking of the Colonel's contribution to physical recreation within the University, Sir Donald handed to the Colonel, as a mark of esteem, a cheque for a substantial sum. 'Thank you indeed,' said the Colonel in reply. 'I am more than grateful for those kind words and also for this handsome cheque — which I now return to you, Sir Donald, in order that it may be ploughed back into the Department of Physical Education.'

For some time he continued to live in the now demolished University house at 54a George Street which entered off Windmill Lane, which had been his home for twenty-two years. In 1952 he discovered that there was an extreme shortage of accommodation in Edinburgh for University staff and, typically, gave up the house, which the University would have allowed him to occupy during his retirement. He continued to be more concerned for the well-being of the young University staff than with his own problems. This was a blow to his friends, but he was keen to live permanently at Salen where he felt he had much unfinished work to do. For a time he kept in touch with his Edinburgh interests. When in the city he stayed at the Overseas Club in Princess Street.

By now he was suffering very badly from a painful hip joint and in 1953 he underwent an operation for the removal of a hip joint and its replacement by a plastic substitute. The operation was technically successful and possibly very necessary, but he was never the same man again. The operation was acutely painful. He said that it was worse than going through three battles and that if he had known what was involved he would never have agreed to surgery. Fortunately it relieved the pain.

The long period of convalescence and remedial exercises in the hospital seemed to unsettle his mind. Later an eye operation in 1955 accelerated the decline of his powers. After the eye operation he was unable to continue to live with his wife alone in the Highlands and the Salen house was sold.

Shortly afterwards Colonel and Mrs Campbell went to lie with their son and daughter-in-law, Niall and Moira, in their house near Bonskeid, Perthshire, a district which held many happy associations for him. He was now badly crippled, almost blind, and his memory was impaired. Nonetheless he struggled on, taking an interest to the best of his ability in his grandchildren and in everything that went on around him.

He received regular visits from his former students and friends and was always anxious to know what was happening in the gym and in the fencing salle. Within the limits of his infirmity he was still thinking far afield and asked searching questions about the causes which were dear to his heart.

His courage never deserted him, nor his 'poker face' flair for the dramatic. When staying with his son at Bonskeid he received a visit from Lord Balerno. As there was no one else at home, he greeted Lord Balerno at the door and ushered him into the drawing room, where a rugby match was being shown on television. 'I'm so glad you can see,' said Lord Balerno, 'I was told that you were almost blind.' 'Poppycock,' retorted the Colonel, 'I see perfectly well. Sit down and enjoy the show, it's a jolly good game.' The two old friends watched the remainder of the match in silence - the Colonel with his back to the television set.

To those who were privileged to know him in his latter days he embodied in his own life the philosophy so carefully worked out in earlier days. As his physical and mental facilities deteriorated the immortal qualities of the spirit shone out from his face to go on into eternity.

Ronald Campbell died on 7th March, 1963 after a short illness. A service at Warriston Crematorium was attended by a large gathering of men and women from all walks of life, many of whom had been greatly influenced by his teaching, and example.

His ashes, together with those of his wife, who died on 6th May, 1965, were scattered by his sons, at Salen, in a clearing high in the surrounding woods which, since the earliest memories of the family, he had called his 'open air Church.' A great warrior and his beloved were at rest.

Acknowledgments

The frontispiece I owe to Colonel Campbell's son, Bruce. For some material, I am indebted to a manuscript history of the Department of Physical Education of the University of Edinburgh, compiled by the late Major Charles Mather and to a manuscript appreciation of Colonel Campbell by his close friend, the late Colonel P.S. Lelean. Colonel Lelean was Professor of Public Health at Edinburgh University. He took a great interest in athletics and never missed an athletic meeting. Part of the chapter on Colonel Campbell's fencing activities is based on an article by Colonel R.A. Hay which appeared in *The Newsletter of the Scottish Amateur Fencing Union* of October 1963.

In addition I have used a number of individual notices which appeared in the press and in various periodicals shortly after Colonel Campbell's death. Among the Colonel's many friends who provided information are
Charles Adams, Edinburgh
J.E.D. Ashe, Charterhouse, London
Lt Colonel A.W. Brocks, Aberdeen
Professor (Emeritus) N. Campbell, Edinburgh
Miss Sheila Cater
Dr D. Collie, London
W.A. Craw, W.S., Edinburgh
Mrs W.M. Dixon, London
Sir Reginald Goodwin, National Association of Boys' Clubs
T.A.K. Hewling, Sheffield
R. Hopkins, London
The late Tom Houston, Edinburgh
L.E. Liddell, Director of Physical Education, Edinburgh University
M.G. Lightfoot, London
F.C.S. Lorimer, National Playing Fields Association
Geoffrey Martin, London
E.W. Pead, London Federation of Boys' Clubs
Dr F. Piercy, Isleworth
Major J.A. Robins, Liss
Colonel The Reverend C.S. Shaw, Adelaide, Campe, South Africa
The late Dr Ian H. Stokoe, Edinburgh
C.J. Tait, Edinburgh
Colonel C.M. Usher, Edinburgh
The late Dr R.E. Verney, Edinburgh
Particular thanks are due to Major T.L. Fletcher, Honorary Curator of the Museum of the Army School of Physical Training at Aldershot and to Ronald D. Lynch, Kent, for their enthusiastic help in supplying the references to the Army School of Physical Training and for directing me to a number of useful articles in the early issues of the school's journal, *Mind, Body and Spirit.*

In Relation to
Physical Education - (Boys & Men)

The Training of BODY, MIND & SPIRIT

in

*FITNESS, TEAMWORK &
SELF-LEADERSHIP*

Life's More Th...
of Blood
It is a Great Spi...

We live in Dee...
In Thoughts
In Feelings, No...
We Should Co...
He Most Lives,...
Who Thinks M...
Acts The Best.

A. BODY

And Though Your Spirit Seem Uncouth or Small,
Stubborn As Clay or Shifting As the Sand,
Strengthen The Body, And the Body Shall
Strengthen The Spirit Till She Take Command:

Be FIT - Be FIT *In Body Next Be Fit*
Rudyard Kipling

IMAGINATIO...
1. Creative-Powe...
2. Ingenuity
3. Initiative
4. Foresight
5. Vision
V
INTELLIGEN...
1. Curiosity
2. Alertness
3. Observation
4. Memory
5. Concentration...
6. Resource
7. Perception
8. Wit
III
THEORY
1. Purpose of Training
2. Application of... Exercises
3. Scope of Trai...
4. Principles of Training
5. Spirit of Trai...
I
B.

VERSATILITY	**VITALITY**
1. Athletics	1. Manliness
2. Field Sports	2. Buoyancy
3. Manual-Labour	3. Personality
4. Craftsmanship	
5. Allotments	
6. Nature Study	
7. Work Camps	
III	IV
TECHNIQUE (PRACTICAL)	**HEALTH**
1. Prowess	1. Robustness
2. Physical	2. Vigour
3. Prestige	3. Cheerfulness
I	II
A. **PHYSICAL ABILITY**	

Edinburgh 18.7.42

art

C. SPIRIT

'A Man's Character is His Destiny'
Heraclitus

Dial
rt-Throbs,

blest,

p James Bailey
Country Town

UDGMENT

iscrimination
rewdness
ict
almness (Balance)
ommon-Sense
isight

VI

DUCATION

ygiene
ietetics
natomy
ysiology
ychology
ology
ilosophy
ociology
ychiatry
holarship

IV

GANISATION

outine
nctuality
diness
)-operation
scipline
xperiment &
Research
atistics

II

RCE

TOLERANCE	NOBILITY
1. Sympathy	1. Appreciativeness
2. Thoughtfulness	2. Unselfishness
3. Comradeship	3. Generosity
4. Understanding	4. Esprit-De-Corps
5. Large-Mindedness	5. Loyality
6. Good-Will	6. Chivalry
7. Good-Humour	7. High-Mindedness
VII	VIII

WILL-POWER	COURAGE
1. Self-Effort	1. Confidence
2. Endurance	2. Independence
3. Self-Reliance	3. Decision
4. Fortitude	4. Self-Sacrifice
5. Resolution	5. Daring-Forthright
6. Concentration	6. Responsibility
7. Steadfastness	
V	VI

ENERGY	SELF-RESTRAINT
1. Self Expression	1. Balance
2. Application	2. Temperance
3. Perserverence	3. Modesty
4. Diligence	4. Patience
5. Enterprise	5. Reserve-Power
6. Drive	6. Stability
III	IV

FAITH	TRUTH
1. Hope	1. Honesty
2. Ambition	2. Sincerity
3. Zest	3. Frankness
4. Reverence	4. Reliability
5. Service	5. Conviction
6. Self-Fulfilment	6. Conscientiousness
7. Inspiration	7. Justice
I	II

C. CHARACTER

Ronald Campbell
18.7.42.

134

Assistance was also received from Newton Chambers & Co Ltd, Sheffield; A.W. Appleton, Bournville Athletic Club; The Director General, Army Medical Services; The Royal Army Medical College; The Home Office; The Ministry of Defence; The Army Records Centre; Captain R. Fogg Elliot, The Gordon Highlanders; Lt Colonel J.E.E. Fry, The Duke of Cornwall's Light Infantry; The Public ARchives of Canada, Department of National Defence, Ottawa; The Boy Scouts Association; The Scottish Association of Boys' Clubs; The London Federation of Boys' Clubs; R.C.B. Stirling, Editor, *The Motherwell Times;* William Brown, Headmaster of Bedford School, and Miss Eileen K. Wade. I have made use of such books as —

General Wauchope by W. Baird
Bedford House: A Diary of Ten Years
The Story of the Royal Tournament by P.L. Binns
Jackets of Green by A. Bryant
The Campbells of Inverawe by I.M. Campbell
Field Marshall Earl Haig by Brig. General J. Charteris
Making Men by W.M. Eagar
The Realities of War by Sir Philip Gibbs
Goodbye to All That by R. Graves
Edgar Wallace by M. Lang
Physical Education in England since 1800 by P.C. McIntosh
The Rugby Union Game by F. Marshall and L.R. Torswill
An Outspoken Soldier by Lt. General Sir Giffard Martel
The Discourses of Dr O'Grady by A. Maurois
The Tragedy of Hector Macdonald by J. Montgomery
The History of the Army Physical Training Corps by Lt Colonel
    E.D.L. Oldfield
Woodbine Willie by W.E. Purcell
Memoirs of an Infantry Officer by S. Sasoon
The Retreat from Mons by Major A.C. Smith
The Soldier who Disobeyed by A.J. Smithers
England's Pride by J. Symons
The Rediscovery of Scotland by G.J. Thomson
An Advanced History of Britain by T.F. Tout
The Sory of Edinburgh University Athletic Club by Colonel C.M.
    Usher
The Chief by E.K. Wade

A special word of thanks is due to Colonel Campbell's two sons, Bruce and Niall, who not only provided me with much useful information but also revised and commented on the manuscripts and proofs.

Finally, a word of thanks to my brother the Reverend Dr Nelson Gray of Scottish Television, my wife Elizabeth, Councillor Magnus Williamson John Cook, former Deputy Director of Education, the Reverend Dr Duncan Shaw and Ian Christie for reading the manuscripts and for their many helpful corrections and suggestions. Also my secretary, Miss Janet Stobie for typing innumerable drafts and who, as always, has proved most helpful.